INSIGHT GUIDES

MADAGASCAR
POCKET GUIDE

◎ Walking Eye App

YOUR FREE EBOOK AVAILABLE THROUGH THE WALKING EYE APP

Your guide now includes a free eBook to your chosen destination, for the same great price as before. Simply download the Walking Eye App from the App Store or Google Play to access your free eBook.

HOW THE WALKING EYE APP WORKS

Through the Walking Eye App, you can purchase a range of eBooks and destination content. However, when you buy this book, you can download the corresponding eBook for free. Just see below in the grey panel where to find your free content and then scan the QR code at the bottom of this page.

Destinations: Download essential destination content featuring recommended sights and attractions, restaurants, hotels and an A–Z of practical information, all available for purchase.

Ships: Interested in ship reviews? Find independent reviews of river and ocean ships in this section, all available for purchase.

eBooks: You can download your free accompanying digital version of this guide here. You will also find a whole range of other eBooks, all available for purchase.

Free access to travel-related blog articles about different destinations, updated on a daily basis.

HOW THE EBOOKS WORK

The eBooks are provided in EPUB file format. Please note that you will need an eBook reader installed on your device to open the file. Many devices come with this as standard, but you may still need to install one manually from Google Play.

The eBook content is identical to the content in the printed guide.

HOW TO DOWNLOAD THE WALKING EYE APP

1. Download the Walking Eye App from the App Store or Google Play.
2. Open the app and select the scanning function from the main menu.
3. Scan the QR code on this page – you will then be asked a security question to verify ownership of the book.
4. Once this has been verified, you will see your eBook in the purchased ebook section, where you will be able to download it.

Other destination apps and eBooks are available for purchase separately or are free with the purchase of the Insight Guide book.

TOP 10 ATTRACTIONS

ANTANANARIVO AND AROUND
Explore the grand palaces and museums that stud the 12 Sacred Hills of Imerina. See page 26.

PARC DE L'ISALO
Sandstone formations and quirky flora characterise this park. See page 43.

PARC NATIONAL DE RANOMAFANA
A dozen lemur and 115 bird species inhabit this biodiverse park's rainforest-swathed slopes. See page 38.

ALLÉE DES BAOBABS
This alley of ancient baobabs is most impressive at dusk. See page 52.

MANDRARE RIVER VALLEY
A spiny forest dominated by the 'octopus tree' offers fabulous lemur-viewing and birdwatching. See page 51.

PARC ANDASIBE-MANTADIA
This park supports many birds, frogs and orchids. See page 32.

MANAMBOLO AND TSIRIBIHINA RIVERS
A boat is the best way to travel towards Morondava. See page 52.

PARC DES TSINGY DE BEMARAHA
The jagged formations of this stone forest support rich flora and fauna. See page 53.

NOSY BE
Dotted with idyllic beaches and lakes, this gorgeous Indian Ocean island also offers snorkelling, whale-watching and lemur-viewing. See page 67.

PARC DE LA MONTAGNE D'AMBRE
Madagascar's oldest park protects nine chameleon species. See page 77.

A **PERFECT** TOUR

Day 1

Antananarivo
Dedicate the morning to the Rova Antananarivo, museums and other old buildings that grace historic Haut-Ville. After a Malagasy-fusion lunch-with-a-view at Restaurant Lokanga, head to the lower town to explore its markets, shops and colonial landmarks.

Days 3-4

Parc National Andasibe-Mantadia
A half-day drive brings you to Madagascar's best one-stop wildlife viewing destination. Take a guided evening walk to see nocturnal tree-frogs, chameleons and lemurs. The next morning, hike into the forested hills in search of the charismatic indri - the largest living lemur. Return to Antananarivo on the second afternoon.

Days 5-6

Baobabs and Tsingy
Fly to the low-key western seaport of Morondava to visit and photograph the iconic Allée des Baobabs, and look for the rare fossa (the island's largest carnivore) in the Réserve Forestière de Kirindy. Allow at least two days to visit the remote Parc National des Tsingy de Bemaraha.

Day 2

Ambohimanga and Ivato
It's about an hour's drive north to Rova Ambohimanga, the most compelling of Imerina's 12 Sacred Hills, with its centuries-old palaces and royal tombs. Head back to suburban Ivato to enjoy a guided tour and pre-booked lunch at La Ferme d'Ivato, then visit the nearby Croc Farm, and stop at Marché Artisanal de la Digue, the island's largest handicraft market.

Days 7-9

Diego Suarez

Fly to the scenic port town of Diego Suarez and base yourself in the lively town centre or at Joffreville on Montagne d'Ambre. A hike in the wildlife-rich forests of Parc National de la Montagne d'Ambre is a must-do. Other great goals for day trips include the historic Montagne des Français, the beach resort of Ramena and the gorgeous La Mer d'Emeraude.

Days 10-11

Réserve Spéciale d'Ankarana

Break the long drive from Diego Suarez to Nosy Be with a short side trip to the surreal Tsingy Rouges and a two-night stay at the Ankarana, the most accessible of Madagascar's major tsingy formations.

Days 14-15

Island-hopping

Follow a morning visit to the steep rainforest-swathed Nosy Komba and its habituated black lemurs with an afternoon snorkelling or diving the multi-coloured coral reefs of Nosy Tanikely. After another night on the island, fly home directly or via Antananarivo.

Days 12-13

Nosy Be

A full-day's drive takes you the lovely tropical island of Nosy Be. Spend the next day chilling out on an idyllic beach or exploring atmospheric Hell-ville. In the late afternoon, head up Mont Passot with its eight crater lakes, to catch the sunset from the summit.

CONTENTS

📖 INTRODUCTION_____10

🏛 HISTORY_____15

📖 WHERE TO GO_____25

Antananarivo_____26
Ville Basse 26, Ville Moyenne 27, Haute-Ville 28, Suburban
highlights 30, Sacred Hills of Imerina 31, Andasibe-Mantadia
and surrounds 32, Lac Itasy 34

Central Highlands_____35
Antsirabe 36, Ambositra 37, Parc National de Ranomafana 38,
Fianarantsoa 40, Ambalavao 41

The Deep South_____42
Parc National de l'Isalo 43, Toliara 43, Ifaty-Mangily 45, Fort
Dauphin 46, The coast east of Fort Dauphin 48, West of Fort
Dauphin 50

The West Coast_____51
Morondava and the Allée des Baobabs 52, Réserve Forestière
de Kirindy 53, Parc National des Tsingy de Bemaraha 53,
Mahajanga 55, Ankarafantsika National Park 56

The Northeast Coast_____57
Canal des Pangalanes 57, Toamasina 59, Foulpointe 61,
Mahambo 62, Île Sainte-Marie 63, Maroantsetra and the
Masoala Peninsula 65, Nosy Be 67, Hell-Ville 68, Beaches 69,
Mont Passot and Lokobe 70 , Other islands 71

The Far North_____73
Diego Suarez 73, Montagne des Français 75, Ramena and the
Emerald Sea 76, Parc National de la Montagne d'Ambre 76,
South of Diego 78

😃 WHAT TO DO _____ 83

Sports and outdoor activities	83
Shopping	93
Entertainment	94
Activities for children	95

😋 EATING OUT _____ 97

🅾 A–Z TRAVEL TIPS _____ 113

🛏 RECOMMENDED HOTELS _____ 134

🌐 INDEX _____ 142

🅾 FEATURES

Fady	14
Jean-Baptiste Lahorde	21
Historical landmarks	23
Indris	34
Chameleons and leaf-tailed geckos	38
Fianarantsoa–Côte Est (FCE) Railway	40
Natural face masks	46
Island of pirates	63
Tsingy	80
Pays Zafimaniry	87
A gentle giant	90
Festivals and events	96
Vanilla	102

INTRODUCTION

Madagascar is unique. Set adrift in the Indian Ocean 500km (300 miles) from Africa and almost 10 times as far from Asia, it is the world's fourth-largest island, extending over some 587,041 sq km (226,658 sq miles), and the most isolated landmass of comparable proportions anywhere in the tropics. Ecologically, it shares the bulk of its DNA with mainland Africa and/or the Indian subcontinent, from which it drifted apart around 160 and 90 million years ago respectively, but its flora and fauna also incorporates wildcard elements from as far afield as South America and Australasia. Culturally, the Malagasy people have equally diverse origins, essentially being a fusion of Indonesian and African stock, liberally spiced with influences from Arabia, India, China, France and elsewhere.

BEACHES, FORESTS AND MOUNTAINS

For many visitors, Madagascar's main attraction is its beaches. The island's 10,000km (6,000-mile) coastline is adorned with idyllic palm-lined beaches, turquoise lagoons, craggy islets and snorkel-friendly coral reefs, and options range from well-developed seaside resorts such as Nosy Be and Ifaty-Mangily to the more uncrowded likes of Île Sainte-Marie and the magnificent Baie de Sainte Luce.

But there is more to Madagascar than beaches. One of the world's top biodiversity hotspots, the island comprises four broad ecological zones. The east and north supports a cover of biodiverse rainforest. The northwest typically supports deciduous forest, while the central highlands host a mosaic of heath, grassland and savannah. Most unique is the semi-arid southwest, whose distinctive flora is referred to as both spiny forest and spiny desert.

LEMURS AND OTHER WILDLIFE

A network of 50-plus national parks and other conservation areas collectively covers around 5 percent of the country's surface area and protects a parallel evolutionary universe comprising an estimated 10,000 endemic animal and plant species:

Carnivorous pitcher plant

more than any other global biodiversity hotspot. The poster-boys for Madagascar's diverse and unique wildlife are the lemurs: a charismatic group of predominantly arboreal primates represented by at least 100 species. Other mammals include 10 carnivores, most notable among them the fossa, which looks like a downscaled puma, but is actually more closely related to the mongoose. For bird enthusiasts, a check-list of almost 290 species includes 105 endemics along with 20 near-endemics.

Guided walks through the national parks of Madagascar provide the opportunity to meet a cast of truly oddball endemics. There are hissing cockroaches, branch-length stick insects, ripe-looking tomato frogs, psychedelically-coloured cat-sized chameleons, camouflaged leaf-tailed geckos, vasa parrots, and comet moths the size of a small bird. But for off-the-wall idiosyncrasy it's difficult to beat the giraffe-necked

Lemurs

Astonishingly, all 100-plus lemur species on Madagascar are thought to be the product of radial evolution from a single colonisation event – most likely a small group of bushbaby-like ancestors that crossed from mainland Africa on floating vegetation – some 30 million years ago.

weevil, which – with its bright red chassis and hinged black neck – doesn't actually resemble a giraffe so much as a miniature crane mounted on a toy fire engine.

A CULTURAL COCKTAIL

An engaging cultural destination, Madagascar was one of the last places on earth to be settled by humans. Most historians agree that the island is unlikely to have been settled any earlier than 500 BC, and that the deep interior remained uninhabited for another 500 years. By the 18th century, its Asiatic and African settlers had merged to form a unique cultural entity dominated by kingdoms such as Imerina, which was ruled from a set of a dozen sacred hills that include Antananarivo and the Rova Ambohimanga, now a Unesco World Heritage Site.

The island's 22 ethno-cultural groups are united in speaking the Malagasy language – which forms part of the Austronesian linguistic group, but is laced with Bantu and other borrowed words – but vary greatly in their traditional cultural practices. Broadly speaking, the main distinction is between the highlanders and the people of the coast. The former, which includes the Merina of Antananarivo as well as the Betsileo, Sihanaka and Zafimaniry, are essentially the descendants of early Indonesian settlers who moved upcountry to take advantage of a climate conducive to cattle-rearing and rice-growing.

By contrast, the coastal peoples have relied more on fishing and maritime trade as their economic mainstays, and also have a more diverse ethnic make-up, thanks to regular injections of fresh African, Arabic, Indian and more recently European stock.

Many facets of traditional Malagasy culture reveal its Indonesian roots. These range from the use of the bamboo-tube *valiha* 'zither' and ubiquity of rice at all meals to the construction of rectangular houses with a central support pillar and sloping roofs. Christianity and Islam both have a strong foothold, but roughly half the Malagasy people adhere to a traditional religion that combines elements of monotheism, ancestral worship and animism. Many cultures hold exhumation rituals, the most famous bring the septennial *famadihana* ('turning of the bones'), which entails removing the embalmed body or bones from the tomb, unwrapping the shroud, then embarking on a period of intense and often joyful communication with the dead ancestor, before the remains are reinterred.

MADAGASCAR TODAY

One of the world's poorest and most undeveloped countries, Madagascar remains predominantly rural, with only 35 percent of the population

Malagasy women in Nosy Be marketplace

living in urban areas, and the remainder mostly eking out an existence as subsistence farmers, cattle-herders or fisher-people. A well-established middle class dates back to the 19th century, but it is very small in numeric terms and largely confined to the capital. Ecologically, aerial photography comparisons suggest that 50 percent of the 75,000 sq km (28,957 sq miles) of indigenous forest present in 1950 is gone, thanks to logging, collection of fuelwood and unmonitored slash-and-burn farming.

Despite this, the fertility of the highlands and east coast ensure that most people are reasonably well fed and a strong sense of community and family means that the island remains relatively crime free. For visitors, the Malagasy people come across as genuinely friendly and hospitable and the opportunity to visit some of the country's protected areas and associated local amenities, makes a vital financial contribution to the conservation of this unique island's habitats and wildlife.

⊘ FADY

A cultural concept to which all visitors should be sensitive is *fady*, a set of taboos enforced by the ancestors. Some taboos are held more-or-less countrywide, for instance pointing a finger at a tomb and any other venerated object, denying hospitality to a stranger, or harming certain species of lemur. Others *fady*s – such as those against swimming, urinating on a mountain slope, or whistling outdoors – are confined to specific locations or clans. Locals who break a *fady* will be shunned as unclean and while some allowances are made for foreigners, a good local guide will ensure that you avoid any major infractions.

A BRIEF HISTORY

Madagascar was one of the last major landmasses to be settled by humans. The earliest unambiguous evidence of permanent habitation dates to around AD 500, and linguistic, genetic and archaeological evidence indicates that these early settlers sailed some 6,000km (4,738 miles) across the Indian Ocean from the Malay Archipelago in outrigger canoes. They were later joined by Swahili settlers from East Africa and merchant sailors from the Arabian Gulf. The island's most important mediaeval settlement was Mahilaka, a walled Muslim city that extended across 60 hectares (150 acres) of mangrove-lined coast close to Nosy Be. The introduction of zebu cattle from mainland Africa c.1000 transformed Madagascar from an agricultural to a mixed pastoral economy. At around the same time, two new clans emerged: the Vazimba (People of the Forest) farmers and hunter-gatherers who abandoned the coast in favour of the fertile but previously unsettled interior, and the nomadic Vezo (People who fish) of the relatively infertile southwest coast.

IMERINA AND EUROPE

The modern history of Madagascar was initiated

Antaisaka warriors, 19th century

Venetian map of Madagascar, 17th century

by the rise of the inland Imerina Kingdom and the arrival of Europeans on the coast. The foundation of Imerina can be dated to the mid-16th century reign of King Andriamanelo, but it took its present form under his successors Ralambo (r.1575–1612) and Andrianjaka (r.1612–30). Imerina experienced its first golden age under a quartet of tongue-twisting monarchs – Andriantsitakatrandriana (r.1630–50), Andriantsi-mitoviaminandriandehibe (r.1650–70), Andrianjaka Razakatsitakatrandriana (r.1670–75) and Andriamasinavalona (r.1675–1710) – but declined after the last of these kings divided it into four sub-realms governed by his four most trusted sons.

Madagascar was first sighted by a Portuguese ship in 1500, but the high incidence of malaria discouraged European settlement until the late 17th century, when the northeast coast served as a base for pirates such as William 'Captain' Kidd. An associated influx of firearms led to an escalation in the slave trade out of Madagascar, the main beneficiaries of which were the coastal kingdoms of Betsimisaraka and Sakalava. Both these kingdoms conducted regular slave raids into the interior, prompting the revival of Imerina under King Andrianampoinimerina (r.1787-1809) and his son Radama I (r.1810-28), who together captured most of the major coastal polities in a series of military campaigns that resulted in devastating loss of life. Radama I consolidated his ascendancy in 1817 by entering into a formal alliance with the British crown that recognised him as King of Madagascar.

Radama I died at the age of 36; exhausted by the long years of war and his insatiable appetite for alcohol; poisoned, say some, by or on behalf of his wife and successor Queen Ranavalona I (r.1828-61). A staunch isolationist, Ranavalona revoked the treaty with Britain, rebuffed French diplomatic approaches, banned her subjects from indulging in Christian practices, and eventually, in 1857, expelled every last foreigner from her realm. Domestically, her reign was marked by her enthusiasm for executing suspected thieves, witches, Christians and other transgressors. Claims that the population of Madagascar halved under Ranavalona I are probably exaggerated, but give some idea of the scale of the killing.

THE BUILD-UP TO COLONISATION

Though short, the reign of Radama II contrasted dramatically with that of his mother, Ranavalona. Within 18 months of his coronation, the young king reopened the country to foreign investment, restored freedom of religion and encouraged foreign settlement. Radama II was assassinated in 1863 and succeeded by his wife Rasoherina, whose most influential act was stripping Prime Minister Rainivoninahitriniony of his position in 1864 and replacing him with his younger brother Rainilaiarivony, who ruled Imerina behind-the-scenes for the next 32 years.

Historically, Madagascar had a closer relationship with England than France. That changed in 1883, when France occupied the northwestern port of Mahajanga and carried a treaty of protectorateship to Antananarivo. Ranavalona II refused

Human impact

Human habitation had a profound ecological impact on Madagascar. Not only did it result in extensive deforestation, but in the extinction of much of its megafauna, notably the immense elephant-bird, the gorilla-sized sloth-lemur, and the once abundant Malagasy hippopotamus.

to sign, so the French took occupation of Toamasina. In December 1885, the stalemate was broken when the recently crowned Ranavalona III and Prime Minister Rainilaiarivony signed a treaty ceding Diego Suarez to France. A tense equilibrium endured until September 1895, when the French bombarded the royal palace, prompting the surrender and exile of Ranavalona III to Algiers, where she died 20 years later.

THE COLONIAL ERA

The nine-year term of the first Governor-General, Joseph Gallieni, was marked by a scorched-earth military policy quelling any anti-colonial resistance. Gallieni also introduced an oppressive corvée system (unpaid peasant labour in lieu of tax) to help fund the colonial administration. During World War II, Madagascar was initially administered by the Vichy Government. In 1942, the Allies captured the entire island and handed it over to the Free French government-in-exile. In 1946, a new constitution recast Madagascar as an overseas territory of France and accorded full citizenship to its inhabitants, but failed to address demands for independence.

The so-called Malagasy Uprising of 1947-8 led to an estimated 89,000 Malagasy civilians being killed. In 1956, France transferred power from Paris to a local parliament elected under universal suffrage. Two main parties contested the first election: Philibert Tsiranana's Parti social-démocrate malgache (PSD), which advocated self-rule within the newly-formed French Community, and the more hardline Antokon'ny Kongresy Fanafahana an'i Madagasikara (AKFM), which favoured severing ties with France and moving towards a socialist economic model. A 1958 referendum voted heavily in favour of the PSD, and Tsiranana was elected president a year later. Madagascar became a sovereign state on 26 June 1960.

POST-INDEPENDENCE

The PSD dominated Malagasy politics between 1960 and 1972. Away from the manipulable polling stations, however, many ordinary Malagasy were suspicious of the PSD and its close relationship with France, anti-communist agenda, high taxation, and inability to stem rising unemployment and falling living standards. Anti-government protests led to Tsiranana's resignation in May 1972. Executive power was transferred to General Ramanantsoa, who won a constitutional referendum suspending civilian government for five years. Ramanantsoa aligned Madagascar with the USSR and nationalised foreign-owned business, which led to food shortages and a rise in corruption. Ramanantsoa resigned in

Malagasy woodworker, Ambositra

Gabriel Ramanantsoa, Head of State from 1972-5

favour of Colonel Richard Ratsimandrava, whose six-day presidency ended when he was assassinated on 11 February 1975.

Ratsimandrava's replacement, Didier Ratsiraka, restored civilian rule, but initially pursued similar policies to his predecessors, leading to the UN listing Madagascar among the world's 20 poorest countries in 1986. Ratsiraka won a third presidential in 1989, but his victory was widely condemned as fraudulent and prompted the formation of the opposition coalition Comité des Forces Vives (CFV) under Albert Zafy. In 1991, the presidential guard gunned down at least 30 demonstrators on the outskirts of Antananarivo, provoking a general strike and, eventually, Ratsiraka's resignation in 1992. Zafy won the 1993 presidential election, but presided over a fractious coalition government that underwent 10 cabinet reshuffles and three changes of prime minister in the space of three years, and was so corrupt that the World Bank, IMF and several other donors suspended aid. Zafy was impeached for corruption, necessitating a December 1996 presidential election that pitted Ratsiraka against him. Ratsiraka won, and his relatively uneventful fourth presidential term coincided with the first period of sustained economic growth since independence.

MADAGASCAR IN THE 21ST CENTURY

In the hotly-contested 2001 presidential election, Ratsiraka, Zafy and three other candidates were beaten by Marc Ravalomanana, the incumbent mayor of Antananarivo, and party leader of Tiako I Madagasikara (literally 'I Love Madagascar', TIM). Ratsiraka initially refused to accept the result and initiated a short but bloody civil war, before fleeing to exile in July 2002.

The first Malagasy president to come from a business background, Ravalomanana worked closely with the IMF and World Bank to improve the transport infrastructure and public

⊙ JEAN-BAPTISTE LABORDE

The most important modernising foreign influence on Madagascar in the 19th century, the engineer Jean-Baptiste Laborde (1805–78) was commissioned by Queen Ranavalona I to transform the swampland below her palace into what is now Lac Anosy (c. 1831) and went on to establish a modern manufacturing complex (including an arms factory, foundry, brickworks and glassmaking centre) at Mantasoa. In 1857, Laborde was exiled from Madagascar due to his involvement in a failed coup to oust Ranavalona I in favour of her son Radama II. He returned as the French consul to Antananarivo following the death of Ranavalona I in 1861. During his two sojourns on the island, Laborde designed several of its best known buildings, among them the original wooden Palais de Manjakamiadana, the tomb of Prime Minister Rainiharo, the wide-balconied wooden house now known as Maison de Jean Laborde, and the two-storey Fandriampahalemana Palace. Laborde died in 1878, was accorded a national funeral, and buried at Mantasoa in a grand tomb, which – in true Malagasy style – he had designed and built himself.

services such as education and healthcare, and to curb government corruption and profligacy.

Having survived attempted two attempted coups, Ravalomanana won another presidential election in December 2006, but his second term was marred by ongoing tensions between himself and Andry Rajoelina, a young media mogul who had been elected mayor of Antananarivo the year before. When Ravalomanana shut down a television channel owned by Rajoelina, the latter initiated a general strike that plunged the country into something close to civil war in January 2009. Ravalomanana tendered his resignation following a military coup on 16 March, and Rajoelina was appointed transitional president. A Southern African Development Community (SADC)-endorsed agreement signed in September 2011 paved the way for a fresh presidential election, but this was delayed until late 2013 while Rajoelina and Ravalomanana were persuaded to withdraw their candidature. The election was eventually won by the Rajoelina-endorsed candidate, Hery Rajaonarimampianina of the Hery Vaovao ho an'i Madagasikara (New Forces for Madagascar) Party.

Now approaching its seventh decade of independence, Madagascar remains one of the world's poorest nations. Between gaining independence in 1960 and 2018, the population has grown fivefold to 25 million, while the per capita GDP has plummeted from US$700 to US$400. Politically, Madagascar has maintained some stability in the aftermath of the 2009 crisis, but ethnic factionalism and petty politics retain the capacity to provoke periods of costly and destructive internal conflict. The next election is due in 2018 and the incumbent's position looks to be far from secure, especially as he will most likely square up against two former presidents in the form of Marc Ravalomanana and Andry Rajoelina likely.

HISTORICAL LANDMARKS

c. **500 AD** Madagascar is settled by Indonesians and soon after by African and Arab seafarers.

1500 The Portuguese navigator Diogo Dias becomes the first European to sight Madagascar.

1643 Jacques Pronis establishes a short-lived French colony at Fort Dauphin.

1685 Adam Baldridge is the first of many pirates to settle near Île Sainte-Marie.

1793 King Andrianampoinimerina of Imerina captures Antananarivo on a drive to extend his realm across the whole island.

1817 Andrianampoinimerina's son Radama I signs a treaty with England recognising him as King of Madagascar.

1896 Madagascar is made a French Colony.

1939–45 Madagascar is placed under the German-allied Vichy. It is captured by Allied Forces in **1942** and handed to the Free French later than year.

1947–8 The Malagasy Uprising leads to 89,000 civilians being killed by the French army.

1960 Madagascar gains independence under Philibert Tsiranana on 26 June.

1975 Under President Ratsiraka, Madagascar severs historic ties with France and adopts socialist policies that lead to economic collapse in the late 1980s.

1993 Ratsiraka is ousted and replaced by Albert Zafy

1997 Zafy is impeached for corruption in 1997, paving the way for Ratsiraka to serve a fourth presidential term.

2001 Marc Ravalomanana is elected president.

2009 Following extensive rioting, Ravalomanana is ousted in a military coup led by Andry Rajoelina.

2013 The first election after the 2009 coup is won by Hery Rajaonarimampianina.

2018 Presidential elections in late 2018 resulted in Rajoelina and Ravalomanana emerging as frontrunners, with a run-off scheduled in December 2018.

Palm trees on the beach, Nosy Be

WHERE TO GO

Exploring Madagascar - the world's fourth-largest island, its vastness exaggerated by a patchy road and rail infrastructure - can be a challenge. But the rewards more than justify the effort.

Most visitors land at the capital, Antananarivo, which stands in the island's centre, half a day's drive from the popular Parc National Andasibe-Mantadia, whose rich lemur diversity includes the adorable diademed sifaka and caterwauling panda-like indri. Surrounded by edifices dating back to the heyday of the Imerina kingdom, Antananarivo is also the hub of a domestic flight network that allows one to reach more remote attractions without losing too much time to road travel.

Madagascar has two main tourist circuits, and visitors with limited time usually stick to one or the other. The lynchpin of the northern circuit is Nosy Be, a popular beach destination that attracts a fair amount of package tourism. Important attractions within striking distance of Nosy Be include the dramatic karstic tsingy landscapes of Ankarana, the endemic-rich rainforest of crater-pocked Montagne d'Ambre, and the charming old harbour city of Diego Suarez.

The southern circuit doesn't lack for luscious beaches, but it is more about active engagement with various cultural, wildlife and scenic attractions. These include the artisanal city of Antsirabe and the Unesco-recognised woodcarving tradition of Pays Zafimaniry, the fluffy lemurs and colourful birds that inhabit the montane forests of Ranomafana, and the stunningly sandstone sculptures of Isalo and spiny forest of the semi-arid southwest.

ANTANANARIVO

Situated at a temperate altitude of 1,280–1,480 (4,200–4,856ft), Madagascar's bustling capital, **Antananarivo ❶** offers an alluring combination of historical sightseeing, French architectural and culinary flair, and modern Malagasy pizzazz. Political centre of Imerina since it was captured by King Andrianjaka c.1610, it now supports a population of roughly 1.6 million. The city itself sprawls across a series of wooded hills and low swampy valleys, which makes for a quaint layout of roads that seem to turn back on themselves, frequently leading newcomers back to the same place they started. Ivato International Airport, 15km (9 miles) from the city centre, is the main port of entry to Madagascar, and the hub of the domestic flight network.

VILLE BASSE

Antananarivo's relatively grid-like **Ville Basse** (Lower City) is essentially a colonial-era CBD established in the early years of the 20th century. Avenue de l'Indépendance, laid out in 1912, is lined with landmark buildings such as the **Hôtel de France ❹** whose wide colonnaded terrace is a good place to watch the city bustle past. At its southeast end, the **Marché des Pavillons d'Analakely ❺** comprises neat rows of oriental-looking red-tiled kiosks that sell everything from fruit and vegetable to clothing, and pirated DVDs. Just past this, jacaranda-shaded Parc d'Ambohijatovo is overlooked by a tall stele commemorating the Malagasy Uprising of 29 March 1947. A prominent landmark at the northwest end of Avenue de l'Indépendance, the handsome **Gare Soarana ❻**, a railway station built in French rural style over 1908–10, now houses a mall and the chic Café de la Gare. About 500m/yards to its southwest, the engaging **Musée des Pirates ❼** (Rue de Liège; Mon–Fri 9am–5pm; charge).

VILLE MOYENNE

Slotting between the commerce-driven CBD and more sedate Haute-Ville in both location and feel, the Middle Town is an administrative quarter focussed on the leafy Jardin d'Antaninarenina which hosts a useful tourist office operated by the Office Régional du Tourisme d'Analamanga (ORTANA; www.tourisme-antananarivo.com; daily 9am–5pm). A block further south, the historic **Hôtel Colbert** 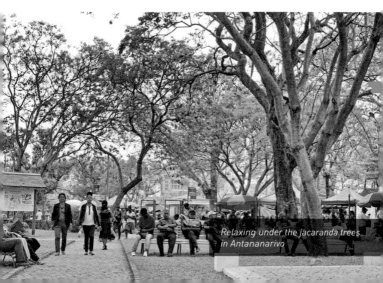 (Rue Printsy Ratsimamanga) first opened its doors in 1940 and its strong period character makes it an excellent place for a drink or meal. Nearby, the ornate facade of the heavily guarded **Palais d'Ambohitsorohitra**, a grand colonial edifice that now doubles as a presidential palace, can be seen from a distance.

Relaxing under the jacaranda trees in Antananarivo

The best known landmark in the Ville Moyenne, heart-shaped **Lac Anosy** ⓕ was established during the reign of Queen Ranavalona I, who commissioned Jean Laborde to fashion an artificial lake from an area of swampland. Since 1927, its island has been the site of a prominent stele dedicated to the Malagasy soldiers who died fighting for France in World War I. From Lac Anosy, you can return to the city centre via the suburb of Isoraka, whose narrow roads house several handsome colonial-era buildings. Isoraka is also the site of the **Musée d'Art et d'Archéologie** ⓖ (Rue Dok Villette; daily 9am–4pm; donation), which includes a small but interesting selection of artefacts from archaeological sites all around the island. About 500 metres/yds west of this, the **Tombeau de Rainiharo** ⓗ is a striking Hindu-influenced arched mausoleum constructed by Jean Laborde in 1852 to house the remains of Prime Minister Rainiharo.

HAUTE-VILLE

Historically the most important part of Antananarivo, **Haute-Ville** occupies the long narrow hill where King Andrianjaka established the first Imerina capital some 400 years ago. Coming from below, you enter the old walled city at Place d'Andohalo, which has served as a public square since the days of King Andrianjaka. It is flanked by the triangular **Jardin d'Andohalo** ⓘ, once the city's main market, later the coronation site of Radama I and subsequent monarchs. Historic buildings near the square include the sandstone **Cathédrale de l'Immaculée Conception d'Andohalo** (inaugurated 1890), the **Maison de Jean Laborde** ⓙ (constructed as a French Embassy in 1863) and the Lycée Gallieni d'Andohal.

Another 300m/yards uphill along Rue Ramboatiana, the **Musée d'Andafiavaratra** ⓚ (Mon–Sat 10am–6pm; charge) is housed in a baroque ridge-top building built in 1876 as the residence of Prime Minister Rainilaiarivony. The museum contains a miscellany of royal paraphernalia, including 19th-century treaties between France and Imerina, traditional astrological artefacts, a jug of royal circumcision water, and oil portraits of Radama I and most subsequent monarchs. Another 100m/yards past this, the **Palais**

Ambatondrafandrana courthouse

de Justice d'Ambatondrafandrana , a courthouse styled like a misplaced Greek Temple, is perched on a natural stone base where the Imerina monarchs once dispensed harsh traditional justice.

The city's highest point is capped by the **Rova Antananarivo** (Mon–Sat 9am–5pm; charge), a residential compound founded by King Andrianjaka c.1610 and partially gutted by fire in 1995. Its centrepiece is the **Palais de Manjakamiadana**, a three-storey palace constructed from hardwood for Queen Ranavalona I over 1839–40, and later encased with a multiple-arched stone facade and quartet of fortress-like turrets under Queen Ranavalona II. Other noteworthy features of the complex include the lovely **Anglican Church** built for Ranavalona II over 1869–80, a cluster of ancient tomb houses including the one built for King Andrianjaka in 1630, and a swimming pool commissioned by Ranavalona III.

Madagascan hoopoe, Tsarasaotra

SUBURBAN HIGHLIGHTS

Situated about 1km (0.6 miles) south of the city centre, the **Parc Botanique et Zoologique de Tsimbazaza** (Rue Kasanga Fernando; http://pbzt.recherches.gov.mg; daily 9am–5pm; charge) contains a largest herbarium, recreations of several different Malagasy habitats, a collection of stone and wooden tomb markers, two ornamental ponds that support a large heronry, a zoo housing half-a-dozen lemur species, and a museum displaying the country's most extensive fossil collection.

The capital's top birdwatching spot, the 5-hectare (12-acre) **Parc Tsarasaotra** (off Colonel Ratsimandrava Parkway; tel: 033-1244127; www.boogiepilgrim-madagascar.com, daily 6am–6pm by appointment; charge) is the only site in the central highlands that offers a decent chance of spotting aquatic endemics such as Meller's duck, Madagascar pond heron and Madagascar grebe.

Set on the banks of the Ikopa Canal halfway along the main road between the city centre and Ivato, the **Marché Artisanal de la Digue P** is Madagascar's largest handicrafts market, comprising more than 100 stalls selling pretty much every conceivable memento and curio.

Some 3km (1.8 miles) past Ivato International Airport, the **Croc Farm Q** (tel: 020-2200715; daily 9am–5pm; charge) is not only an active crocodile farm but it also supports free-ranging populations of (introduced) Coquerel's sifaka and several (naturally occurring) aquatic birds, while open-air cages house tortoises, snakes, chameleons and other reptiles. A visit could be combined with a tour of **La Ferme d'Ivato R** (tel: 032-1159495/6; www.lafermedivato.com; daily 10am–3pm by appointment; charge), a working farm that specialises in organic produce and also has a great rustic restaurant.

SACRED HILLS OF IMERINA

Antananarivo stands at the heart of Imerina, a powerful highland kingdom centred on 12 sacred hills. The most important of these, inscribed by Unesco as the island's only cultural World Heritage Site in 2001, is the **Rova Ambohimanga S** (www.ambohimanga-rova.com; daily 9am–4pm; charge), a forested rocky outcrop that stands some 23km (14 miles) north of central Antananarivo.

Ambohimanga is entered via **Ambatomitsanaga Gate**, which features an excellent example of a *vavahady*, a traditional circular stone disc door that would be rolled into place by several dozen slaves when the complex was under threat. Within the main compound stands **Mahandrihono Palace**, a single-roomed one-storey wooden structure built in 1788 by King Andrianampoinimerina, together with a pair of more elaborate two-storey buildings that once formed the summer residence of Queen Ranavalona II. The wooden

Golden frogs

More than 100 endemic frog species have been recorded within 30km (18 mile) of Andisibe village. The flagship species is the endangered golden mantella (Mantella aurantiaca), a tiny (up to 25mm/1 inch) critter named for its bright gold (or occasionally orange) colour.

tombs of two queens and three kings are lined up behind the latter like a row of windowless beach huts. A 3–4 hour guided walking trail around the forested hill takes in two smaller royal compounds, the fern-covered Grottes d'Andranomatsatso, the sacred Lac d'Amparihimasina, and Andakana Gate, the most interesting of the ancient vavahady stone disc entrances to the royal hill.

East of Ambohimanga, the little-visited **Rova Ambohidrabiby** ❶ (daily 9am–4pm; donation) has a strong claim to being the oldest capital of Imerina. Literally translating as Hill of Rabiby, Ambohidrabiby is named after Ralambo's grandfather, an Arab astrologer who arrived there from the coast circa 1520 and and had his name bastardised to Rabiby. The site incorporates the stone tombs of Rabiby and Ralambo, and a small museum.

Now a small forested suburban enclave situated to the northeast of central Antananarivo, **Rova Ilafy** ❶ (daily 9am–noon and 2–5pm) was founded in 1861 as the part-time capital of King Radama II, who was buried there upon his death two years later. The two-storey wooden house built for Radama II is now an excellent ethnographic museum boasting a collection of traditional musical instruments and funerary totems.

ANDASIBE-MANTADIA AND SURROUNDS

The most convenient one-stop wildlife destination in Madagascar, **Parc National Andasibe-Mantadia** ❷ (www.

parcs-madagascar.com; daily 6am–4pm; charge), less than half a day's drive east of Antananarivo, is the main strong-hold of the indri, the largest of all living lemurs. Other wildlife includes diademed sifaka, giant bamboo lemur, black-and-white ruffed lemur and Goodman's mouse lemur, along with 110 bird species and a wide variety of nocturnal lemurs, cha-meleons and tree-frogs.

The national park has two disjunct components. The smaller **Réserve Spéciale d'Analamazaotra** extends across 8 sq km (3 sq miles) of lushly forested hills near Andasibe village and is traversed by two short guided trails that offer a great chance of seeing (indri and other lemurs. Bordering Analamazaotra, indris are also likely to be seen on guided hikes through the 7-sq-km (2.7-sq-mile), **Parc Mitsinjo** (https://association-mitsinjo.wordpress.com; daily 7am–4pm; charge).

Parc Mitsinjo is the base for Across Branch, an organisation that offers zip-lining from a 25-metre (82ft) -high platform along a 100 metre (330ft) cable starting, and climbing a tree 15m (50ft) into a canopy to relax in a ham-mock and look for wildlife (including indris). **Parc Voi MMA** (daily 7am–4pm; charge) is a tiny (32-hectare/79-acre) is another community-based reserve whose guides are

Coquerel's sifaka lemur in Andasibe-Mantadia

adept at locating localised birds such as Madagascar wood rail, Madagascar crested ibis, red-breasted coua, Madagascar long-eared owl and Madagascar pygmy kingfisher.

Larger and more ecologically diverse that Analamazaotra, **Parc National de Mantadia** (www.parcs-madagascar.com; daily 6am–4pm; charge) extends for roughly 158 sq km (61 sq miles) across a sequence of forested hills which start to the north of Andasibe village. Mantadia protects almost all the vertebrate species found in Analamazaotra, along with plenty that aren't – notably the black-and-white ruffed lemur. However, its relatively remote location means it is far less frequented, except by dedicated birdwatchers.

LAC ITASY

Some 25km (165 miles) west of the central Antananarivo, **Lemurs' Park** ⓥ (www.lemurspark.com; daily 9am–5pm; charge) is a great place to see free-ranging populations of

⊙ INDRIS

The panda-like indri is distinguished from the related sifakas by a combination of greater bulk, big yellow eyes, large tufted ears and stumpy tail. Among the most strictly arboreal of lemurs, it feeds almost exclusively on leaves and seldom descends from the trees. A unique feature of the indri is its loud and distinctive call. Madagascar's largest living primate, the indri is only a fraction of the size of the extinct *Archaeoindris*, a robust tailless terrestrial lemur that would have weighed around 160kg (350lb; larger than an adult female gorilla) and became extinct over the last 2,000 years as a result of resultant habitat loss and predation following the arrival of humans.

seven introduced diurnal lemur species. Another 96km (59 miles) to the west, the 35 sq km (13.5 sq miles) **Lac Itasy**  is the island's third largest lake, and easily explored by canoe or on foot. An interesting goal for a day outing is the **Îlot Sacré Ambohiniazy**, which houses the tomb of the 17th-century King Andriambahoaka and is also the site of an impressive fruit bat colony. Also in the vicinity of Itasy are the surreal **Geysers d'Andranomandraotra** ❸, which spout up to 50cm (20 ins) into the air from a fantastic stalagmite-like quartet of tufa mounds, and the lovely 20-metre (65ft) -high **Chutes de la Lily** ❻.

Canoes on Lac Itasy

CENTRAL HIGHLANDS

The highland region to the south of Antananarivo is one of the few parts of Madagascar that can be explored with relative ease by car, since it is bisected by surfaced 980km (609 miles) RN7 between the capital and the port of Toliara. The RN7 offers direct or indirect access to several key attractions, from national parks such as Ranomafana and Isalo to the historic old towns of Antsirabe and Fianarantsoa. Theoretically, you could cover its full length in two days of daylight driving, but if sightseeing is a priority, then allocate at least a week to 10 days, to the trip.

ANTSIRABE

Situated 170km (105 miles) south of Antananarivo, **Antsirabe ❸** means 'Place of Big Salt', a name that dates back hundreds of years, to when it was just a small market village renowned for selling salt extracted from its potash-rich soils and thermal springs. Today, it is Madagascar's third-largest city, with a population of 250,000, and an unusually vibrant feel thanks to its thriving industrial sector and the surrounding fertile and well-watered volcanic soils. It is particularly worth visiting on Saturday mornings, when the colourful open-air **Tsena Sabotsy** (Saturday market), set in a large walled hilltop compound on the southwestern outskirts, is at its busiest and most chaotic.

Antsirabe is renowned for its artisanal enterprises. **Maminirina Corne de Zébu** (Parc de l'Est; daily 7am–7pm; free), is an ingenious cottage industry dedicated to manufacturing richly-textured and multihued souvenirs from zebu horns. Visitors are treated to a free demonstration of the process used to transform the horns into a malleable sculpting material used to make artefacts ranging from salad bowls, drink coasters and ashtrays to pretty jewellery and figurines of lemurs and birds. Next door, the **Broderie et Miniature Mamy** (Parc de l'Est; Mon–Sat 8am–6pm;

Turning zebu horn into ornaments and jewellery

free), founded in 1990, manufactures and sells miniature cars, bicycles, rickshaws and other items made from recycled metal.

A popular outing from Antsirabe leads to two pretty crater lakes: **Lac Andraikiba**, 7km (4 miles) west of town, and the smaller and steeper-sided **Lac Tritriva** 10km (6 miles) further southwest. Walking trails run around

Wild silk

Soatanana is a stronghold for the tapia tree, staple diet and breeding ground of the endemic Madagascar silkworm, whose cocoons, harvested over March to June, produce a unique and highly prized 'wild silk', darker in colour and more textured than the one associated with the domestic silkworm.

both lakes but locals say that those who transgress an ancient *fady* on swimming in Lac Tritriva will drown. Either or both form an excellent goal for a bicycle or scooter trip out of Antsirabe.

AMBOSITRA

Sprawling attractively across a patchwork of paddy-flanked hills 92km (55 miles) south of Antsirabe, **Ambositra** ❹ – literally 'Place of Many Zebus' - is best-known today as the centre of the unique Zafimaniry wood-crafting tradition. The town's winding alleys are lined with craft shops selling wooden sculptures, many housed in colonial buildings whose intricately carved balconies are another facet of the Zafimaniry legacy. A pleasant 4km (2.5 miles) drive or walk southwest of the town centre leads to the **Rova Ambositra**, an 18th-century palace built by the Betsileo monarch Mpanalina II. The original was all but destroyed by King Radama in 1811, but the two main wooden buildings, both ornately carved with a tiled roof, have since been restored. Ambositra is also the springboard for hikes in the remote mountains of the **Pays Zafimaniry**.

A picturesque village of earthy traditional two-storey Merina houses surrounded by tall granite outcrops, **Soatanana**, 40km (24 miles) southwest of Ambositra, produces some of the country's finest handcrafted silk scarves and other products on traditional wooden looms. Local guides will demonstrate the silk-production process from start to end, and it's an excellent place to buy hand-crafted silkware direct from source.

PARC NATIONAL DE RANOMAFANA

One of Madagascar's most popular and biodiverse protected areas, **Parc National de Ranomafana 5** (www.parcs-mada-gascar.com; daily 7am–4pm; charge) protects 416 sq km (160 sq miles) of lush rainforest-swathed slopes flanking

⊘ CHAMELEONS AND LEAF-TAILED GECKOS

Half the world's 200-odd chameleon species are endemic to Madagascar. Oustalet's and Parson's chameleons, which regularly attain a body length of 60cm (2ft), vie with each other for the title of world's largest chameleon, while the slightly smaller panther chameleon takes the gong when it comes to uninhibited gaudiness. By contrast, reptiles don't come any more diminutive than the astonishing *Brookesia micra*.

Less familiar than chameleons, the leaf-tailed geckos of the endemic genus *Uroplatus* are equally bizarre, with their wide eyes, large colourful mouths, delicate fingers, spatulate tails, and capacity to render themselves near invisible to diurnal predators. Most extraordinary in this respect is the mossy leaf-tailed gecko, with its lichen-like green, grey and brown scaling, and frilled underparts that erase any shadow when it is flattened against a tree.

the RN25 about 20km (12 miles) east of its junction with the RN7 and almost 400km (240 miles) south of Antananarivo. It is home to 12 species of lemur, including the critically endangered golden bamboo lemur, as well as 115 bird species. The most popular day trails – and best for general lemur viewing – are the 15km (9-mile) **Circuit de Varibolema** and 11km (7-mile) **Circuit de Edena**,

Leaf-tailed gecko

both of which start at Varibolo Ticket Office.

Situated alongside the RN25 60km (37 miles) east of Ranomafana, the Kianjavato Research Station (tel: 032-0378008; https://madagascarpartnership.org; charge) was established to protect and study Jolly's mouse lemur, an endangered species named after the pioneering primatologist Alison Jolly. It also harbours a population of habituated aye-ayes that offer the best opportunity in Madagascar of seeing these perversely charismatic creatures in the wild.

Another 115km (70 miles) southeast of Kianjavato, **Manakara ⑥** is a sleepy port town set on an attractive stretch of coast at the coastal terminus of historic and scenic Fianarantsoa–Côte Est railway line. It is a pleasant place but a more attractive option than staying in town is to head 8km (5 miles) south to Club Vanille, which stands on an idyllic and undeveloped beach sandwiched between the open sea and a canal.

FIANARANTSOA

Situated 410km (246 miles) south of Antananarivo, **Fianarantsoa ❼** is Madagascar's fifth-largest city, with a population estimated at 200,000. Its main point of interest is Haute-Ville, which resembles a scaled-down variation on its namesake in Antananarivo. The old town incorporates 500 houses constructed between 1868 and the turn of the 20th century, many occupied by the descendants of their original inhabitants. The **Cathédrale d'Ambozontany** is an imposing brick-faced Catholic edifice constructed in 1890, while the nearby FJKM Antranobiriky and FLM Trinitie Masombahoaka are more modest Protestant churches that respectively date back to 1859 and 1885.

A popular overnight base or lunch stop in the vicinity of Fianarantsoa, the artificial **Lac Sahambavy** is overlooked by the legendary Lac Hôtel and home to the 330ha (815 acre) Sidexam Tea Estate (Mon–Fri 9am–4pm; charge).

◎ FIANARANTSOA-CÔTE EST (FCE) RAILWAY

Laid over 1926–36 using narrow-gauge 19th-century German rails awarded to France as World War I reparation, the 163km (102 mile) FCE line navigates an incredible 48 tunnels and 65 bridges along its spectacular descent from the highland town of Fianarantsoa to the port of Manakara. In theory, coast-bound trains leave Fianarantsoa at 7am on Tuesday and Saturday, taking anything from 12 to 24 hours to complete the journey, and the return trip out of Manakara departs at 7am on Wednesday and Sunday. The trip is only worth considering if you've a reasonably flexible schedule, and it is emphatically worth paying extra to travel first-class.

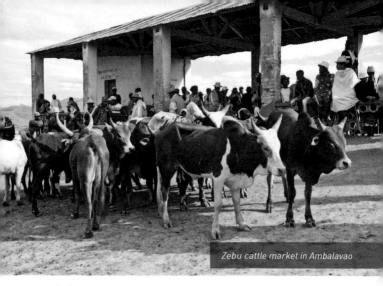
Zebu cattle market in Ambalavao

AMBALAVAO

A steep 54km (32-mile) descent along the RN7 from Fianarantsoa leads to **Ambalavao ❶**, a neat town of 30,000 set in a hilly basin intermediate in feel between the moist high-lands to the north and the drier low country to the south. Every Wednesday, Ambalavao hosts the country's largest livestock market, a vibrant and exciting event that runs from dawn to dusk. At other times, the main attraction within the town limits is the Atelier Soalandy (daily 7am–5pm; free), which offers fascinating 20-minute demonstrations of silk production. Around 4km out of town along the road from Fianarantsoa, the renowned Soavita Wincry (Mon–Sat 7–11am and 1–5pm; charge) offers informative and enjoyable wine-making and -tasting tours.

Alongside the RN7, 12km (7 miles) west of Ambalavao, the 37ha (91 acre) **Réserve d'Anja** (http://anjareserve.angelfire.com; daily 7am–5pm; charge) is a community reserve that protects

The mountains of Parc National d'Andringitra

a pocket of natural forest at the base of an imposing domed granite inselberg. It was set aside to protect a population of ring-tailed lemurs that has increased from around 150 individuals to an estimated 400 since 1999. Guided walks are best undertaken in the early morning or late afternoon, when these most monkey-like of lemurs often sun themselves on the rocks or come to the reservoir to drink.

Situated 47km (28 miles) south of Ambalavao, the 311-sq-km (120-sq-mile) **Parc National d'Andringitra ⑨** (www.parcs-madagascar.com; daily 6.30am–3.30pm; charge) protects an eponymous granite massif that supports more than 50 mammal species, the most of any protected area in Madagascar. Andringitra is traversed by five hiking trails that collectively explore all its major habitats. Most challenging and popular with peak-baggers, the **Circuit d'Imarivolanitra** is a 28km (17 mile) two-day round hike that leads to the 2,658-metre (8,720ft) summit of **Pic Boby**, the country's second-tallest peak (and the highest that can be scaled without specialist climbing gear).

THE DEEP SOUTH

From Ambalavao, the RN7 descends into a lower-lying and more arid famed for the unique succulent-dominated flora of the so-called spiny desert. The most popular and easily visited sites in the region are the wildly scenic Parc National de l'Isalo and pleasant port of Toliara, both of which are served by the RN7. Other more remote sites most easily reached by air include Fort Dauphin and the Mandrare River Valley.

PARC NATIONAL DE L'ISALO

Bisected by the RN7 between Ambalavao and Toliara (see page 43), the **Parc National de l'Isalo** ❿ (www.parcs-madagascar. com; daily 6.30am–4.30pm; charge) was gazetted in 1999 to protect a 815-sq-km (314 sq-mile) tract of semi-arid grassland from which a vast massif of contorted water- and wind-eroded sandstone formations rises to a maximum altitude of 1,268 metres (4,160ft). The evocative rockscapes of Isalo include all manner of otherworldly eroded strata and spine-like formations dotted with jagged peaks and balancing rocks, and support a wealth of suitably bizarre succulents, including the bulbous elephant's foot *Pachypodium rosulatum*. Verreaux's sifaka, red-fronted brown lemur and ring-tailed lemur are all easily seen on guided day hikes guides from the main park entrance in **Ranohira**. The most popular option is a 12km- (7-mile), four-hour circular day hike to a beautiful palm fringed natural swimming pool set oasis-like near the base of the rocky massif. Next to the RN7, 15km (9 miles) west of Ranohira, the **Reine de l'Isalo** is a spectacular roadside balancing rock formation now scarred by graffiti. Just past this, a short dirt track runs north to **La Fenêtre de l'Isalo**, an elevated rock arch that offers very photogenic views at sunset.

TOLIARA

The timeworn seaport of **Toliara** ⓫ stands on the south-west coast 10km (6 miles) north of the Tropic of Capricorn

Moor your boat there

Toliara is often referred to by the pre-1975 French spelling Tuléar. Both derive from the Malagasy phrase *toly eroa*, which an early maritime visitor misunderstood to be a place name rather than generic advice to 'moor your boat there'.

and 5km (3 miles) south of the sandy Fiherenana Delta. The city supports a population of 200,000, but unemployment is high, and it possesses a distinct aura of end-of-the-road tropical ennui. Sightseeing is limited. The **Musée Cedratom** (Rue Philibert Tsiranana; Mon–Sat 7.30–11.30am; Mon–Sat 7.30–11.30am and 2.30–5.30pm; charge) contains a small but interesting ethnographic collection dominated by funerary items. South of the town centre, the **Musée de la Mer** (Avenue de France; Mon–Sat 8am–noon and 2.30–5.30pm; charge) accords museum pride of place goes to half-a dozen stuffed specimens of coelacanth, a hefty 'living fossil' caught off the shore of Toliara on several occasions.

On the south side of the RN7 12km (7 miles) southeast of central Toliara, the highly worthwhile **Arboretum d'Antsokay** (www.antsokayarboretum.org; 7.30am–5.30pm; charge) was established in 1980 to help protect the unique succulent-dominated flora of southwest Madagascar. A labelled botanical trail introduces visitors to some of the southwest's more interesting plants, including the 'European tree' *Commiphora apprevalii*, whose bark peels like sunburnt skin, and the velvet elephant-ear *Kalanchoe beharensis*, also known as Napoleon's hat on account of its unusual shape. The checklist of 30-plus bird species includes running and red-capped coua, and night walks can be arranged. A good interpretative centre and restaurant are attached.

IFATY-MANGILY

The twin villages of **Ifaty** and **Mangily** ⑫ lie about 25km (15 miles) north of Toliara on a lovely stretch of coast accessed along the newly surfaced RN9. The area's white sandy beach, protected by offshore reefs and lined with swaying palms and casuarinas, offer safe swimming, and accommodate a compact cluster of agreeably laidback restaurants and bars. Ifaty and Mangily stand on the shallow **Baie de Ranobe**, a marine biodiversity hotspot that offers great conditions for snorkelling and scuba diving on coral formations inhabited by dense populations of colourful reef fish as well as moray eels, electric rays and marine turtles.

Mangily is home to a cluster of private terrestrial reserves. The **Réserve de Reniala** (https://reniala-ecotourisme.jimdo.com; daily 5.30am–5.30pm; charge is named after the hundreds of ancient fony baobabs that dominate its 60 hectares (148 acres) of spiny forest. Guided walks take up to 90 minutes and offer a possibility of seeing sportive lemurs and various localised birds. Almost adjacent to Reniala and protecting a broadly similar habitat of spiny forest, **Parc Musa** (tel: 033-1913928; daily 5am–5pm; charge) and **Forêt de Baobabs** (tel: 034-7199921; daily

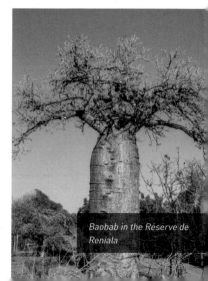

Baobab in the Réserve de Reniala

6am–6.30pm; charge) are better suited to birdwatchers as their guides pay special attention to locating half-a-dozen avian species whose range is more-or-less restricted to the far southwest.

FORT DAUPHIN

Situated at the base of Pic St Louis, the isolated seaport of **Fort Dauphin** ⑬ (or Tôlanaro), perched on a wildly beautiful peninsula has the agreeable feel of a transplanted French seaside village. It was founded in 1643 by Jacques Pronis and today, agriculture, tourism and mining are all important to the local economy, but development is hampered by poor road access – in the rainy season, it can take three days to cover the 500km (300-mile) RN13 connecting Fort Dauphin to Ihosy

◎ NATURAL FACE MASKS

In most coastal regions of Madagascar, but particularly around Toliara, you'll regularly encounter women whose faces are painted with a thick layer of white, yellowish or orange paste. This is not some sort of ritual adornment, but a cosmetic beauty mask that enhances the wearer's immediate appearance whilst also helping to soften the skin and protect it from the sun. The paste is created by rubbing the bark of the mason-joany (sandalwood) tree *Santalina madagascariensis* against a coral stone to produce a fine powder, then adding water and possibly a natural floral extract for colour. The origin of this practice is unknown, but the fact it is most widespread on the west coast, and a similar paste called *musiiro* is applied by the Makua people on the facing north Mozambican coast, suggests it is rooted on the African mainland.

on the RN7, and the longer coastal route from Toliara via Cap Sainte-Marie is even slower. For all but the most hardy of travellers, this means that access is essentially limited to daily flights from Antananarivo.

Fort Dauphin's one notable historic landmarks is the **Musée du Fort Flacourt** (Avenue Gallieni; Mon–Sat 9–11.30am and 2.30–5pm; no photography; charge) which is housed in the original fort built

Fort Flacourt, Tôlanaro

by Governor Etienne de Flacourt in 1648, and contains some interesting colonial-era photographs and maps, and musical instruments and other artefacts relating to the local Antanosy culture. A delightful scenic walk follows the clifftop Rue de la Corniche south out of town for 1.5km (1 mile) to the south end of the hammerhead and the pretty **Plage de Libanona**, which stretches for 500 metres/yds along a curving sandy bay that's usually safe for swimming, though strong currents can pose a genuine threat. A less sheltered suburban beach, but better for surfing, **Plage d'Ankoba** lies on Fausse Baie des Galions about 2km (1.2 miles) west of the town centre, on the south side of Rue Circulaire as it runs towards the airport.

Flanking the RN12a 2km (1.2 miles) north of the SIFOR Factory, the **Parc Botanique de Saïadi** (www.madagascar-resorts.com; daily 8am–5pm; charge) offers the opportunity to walk and canoe through 20 hectares (50 acres) of landscaped lush gardens that support a variety of orchids and birds as well as introduced larger wildlife such as ring-tailed lemur and Nile crocodiles. Only 2km (1.2 miles) north of Saïadi, the similar and in most respects superior **Réserve de Nahampoana** (www. nahampoana.com; daily 8am–5pm; charge) is an attractively landscaped and well-maintained former botanical garden that extends over 50 hectares (123 acres) and hosts introduced but free-ranging (and very tame) troops of Verreaux's sifaka, ring-tailed lemur and brown lemur.

THE COAST EAST OF FORT DAUPHIN

The coastline immediately northeast of Fort Dauphin comprises a narrow 12km (8 mile) long network of shallow lakes and interconnecting channels. Starting at the western shore

Plage de Libanona, Fort Dauphin

of **Lac Lanirano**, only 3km (2 miles) from Fort Dauphin by road, it is possible to take a local pirogue all the way east via the Lac Ambavarano to the spectacular **Evatraha Peninsula**. It's a lovely trip, gliding through an ethereal landscape of brackish inky black channels covered in floating vegetation and flanked by odd low palm-like plants and white-barked mangroves that harbour plenty of herons and other aquatic birds. When you disembark at the Evatraha Peninsula, you can either walk 2.5km (1.5 miles) south to **Pointe d'Evatraha**, which offers wonderful views across the 10km (6.2-mile) -long Baie de Farodafay to Fort Dauphin, or hike 3km (2 miles) north to the gorgeous sheltered beach at the **Baie de Lokaro**. The full-day outing takes around two hours each way by boat, and at least 30 minutes in either direction on foot, so an early start is advised.

Some 40km (24 miles) northeast of Fort Dauphin (a two-hour drive along the unpaved and undulating RN13a), the **Baie de Sainte Luce ⑭**, is one of the most beautiful and isolated stretches of coastline anywhere in Madagascar. Its main terrestrial attraction is the **Sainte Luce Reserve** (tel: 034-9317588; www.sainte-luce-reserve.com), a community-based project founded in 2009 to conserve 17 pockets of east coast littoral forest with a total extent of 13.6 sq km (5.25 sq miles). Inhabitants include the endangered collared brown lemur, and an extensive checklist of forest birds including Madagascar crested ibis, giant coua and Madagascar pygmy kingfisher (the latter often seen on night walks). Guided walks into the largest of the reserve's forest blocks (Sector 9) can be arranged out of the rustic Antanosy village of Manafiafy. In tourist terms, Sainte Luce is more-or-less synonymous with **Manafiafy Lodge** (tel: 020-2202226; www.madaclassic.com), an exclusive beach idyll that offers snorkelling excursions off a nearby coral-fringed beach, kayaking between the rocky islands, motorboat trips into the mangroves, and seasonal whale-watching.

WEST OF FORT DAUPHIN

Set in the western foothills of **Pic St Louis** 11km (7 miles) from central Fort Dauphin, the 125-hectare (310-acre) Domaine de la Cascade (tel: 032-0767823; www.domainedelacascade.net; charge) is reached by following the RN13 to Manatantely, then turning right onto a well-signposted 1.5km (1-mile) dirt feeder road. This private estate, complete with large vanilla and lychee plantation, as well as 50 honey-producing beehives, is named after a small but pretty waterfall that can be reached in two hours along a well-laid footpath. It also contains patches of primary forest, two natural swimming pools, attractively rustic accommodation and a small restaurant. Wildlife includes Verreaux's sifaka, brown lemur and various forest birds.

Past Ranopiso, 40km (24 miles) west of Fort Dauphin, the RN13 skirts what is by far the smallest and also comfortably the most accessible of the three disjunct sectors that comprise the 760-sq-km (293-sq-mile) **Parc National d'Andohahela** ⓰ (www.parcs-madagascar.com; daily 7.30am–5.30pm; charge), which was set aside as a strict nature reserve in 1939 and made a national park in 1988. The transitional moist forest in this small sector of the park covers a mere 5 sq km (2 sq miles) but is the only place in the world with a naturally occurring population of the unusually-shaped triangle palm *Dypsis decaryi* (which, though widely cultivated elsewhere, is represented by no more than 1,000 specimens in the wild. Three guided trails run into Andohahela from a prominent ticket office on the RN13 about 5km (3 miles) west of Ranopiso. The most popular option is the 3.7km (2-mile) **Circuit de Tsimelahy**, which leaves from the village of the same name, passes through some interesting vegetation (including

many triangle palms) and offers a good chance of spotting Verreaux's sifaka and ring-tailed lemur.

The most compelling attraction in the vicinity of Fort Dauphin, and primary reason for most tourist visits, is the **Mandrare River Valley** ⓰, a tract of 'spiny forest' run through by the eponymous river - the largest in southern Madagascar - about four hours' drive further west. Heavily planted with sisal, the spiny forest here is less pristine than similar semi-arid habitats further west, but it is also the main home of the surreal landscape's most eye-catching feature, the bizarre multi-ten-drilled 'octopus tree' *Didierea madagascariensis*. Tourists have a choice of two largely self-sufficient goals: the world-famous **Réserve de Bérenty** and the rather more upmarket Mandrare River Lodge (tel: 020-2202226; www.madaclassic.com) Both locations offer a great opportunity to see the endearing ring-tailed lemur, the dancing Verreaux's sifaka, and a long list of localised avian endemics including giant coua, running coua, subdesert brush-warbler and thamnornis-warbler.

THE WEST COAST

The most iconic landmark on the west coast of Madagascar is the photogenic Allée des Baobabs near the port of Morondava.

Boat safaris

An adventurous way to travel to Morondava is a multiple-day cruise on the Tsiribihina or Manambolo rivers. Though less established, the latter is more exciting, as it threads through an imposing sandstone gorge frequented by sifakas en route to the Tsingy de Bemaraha.

The region is also host to some exceptional protected areas, notably Parc National des Tsingy de Bemaraha and its spectacular karstic rock-scapes, and the Réserve Forestière de Kirindy, the most reliable site for seeing fossa. Further north, the historic port of Mahajanga is the air gateway to the vast Parc National d'Ankarafantsika and several other beauty spots.

MORONDAVA AND THE ALLÉE DES BAOBABS

Situated on the west coast 660km (400 miles) by road from Antananarivo, sleepy **Morondava** ⑰ has is an old port town set on a virtual island bounded on all sides by ocean, canal or marshland. Only 30 minutes' drive to the northeast, the **Allée des Baobabs** is a short stretch of road lined on either side by two dozen centuries-old Grandidier's baobabs, the highest of which stands 30m (98ft) tall. The avenue is best visited at dusk, when the trees' smooth trunks glow orange-brown in the golden light, and the formation silhouettes photogenically against the setting sun. Only 7km (4.3 miles) further northwest, the intertwined trunks of the **Baobabs Amoureux** comprises a pair of Adansonia za baobabs that legendarily contain the spirits of two star-crossed lovers who were forced into an arranged marriage, but reincarnated locked together in an eternal embrace after their death.

RÉSERVE FORESTIÈRE DE KIRINDY

A privately-managed forest reserve situated 65km (39 miles) north of Morondava, the **Réserve Forestière Kirindy** 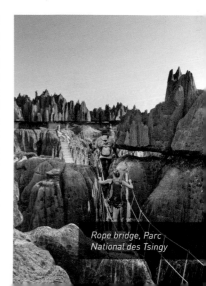 is the most reliable site for seeing the fossa, a striking nocturnal hunter that's most conspicuous during the mating season (September to November). It is also a stronghold for the Malagasy giant rat, an oddball endemic that grows as large as a rabbit, leaps a metre (3ft) into the air to escape predators, and has a total range of 20-sq-km (7-sq-mile). Guided day walks offer a good chance of spotting several of the 45 bird, 30 reptile and seven lemur species recorded to date, but you need to spend at least one night in the basic camp to stand a solid chance of encountering fossa or giant rat.

PARC NATIONAL DES TSINGY DE BEMARAHA

Inscribed as a Unesco World Heritage Site in 1990, the remote **Parc National des Tsingy de Bemaraha** lies 190km (115 miles) north of Morondava along a rough dry-season-only road that takes a full day to cover in a private 4x4, and at least two days by taxi-brousse. Ample justification for this energy-sapping drive comes in the form of the so-called **Grand Tsingy**, a labyrinthine karstic

Rope bridge, Parc National des Tsingy

Rocky overhang, Manambolo River

formation of jagged black limestone pinnacles that stretches almost 100km (60 miles) from north to south. Despite being referred to as a stone forest, Bemaraha possesses many desert-like qualities, with daytime temperatures on the exposed stone canopy frequently soaring above 50°C (122°F) and what little rain does fall tending to put straight down the bare rock slopes into tall narrow valleys up to 100m (330ft) deep. Inhospitable as it might look, this jagged rock archipelago supports a xerophile flora and fauna as diverse as it is predictably rich in endemics, most famously the magnificent Von der Decken's sifaka, which has a creamy-white coat offset by a black face mask and prominent yellow eyes, and is often seen crossing the tsingy pinnacles in small family parties.

Although 4x4 trails run through the park, it is best explored on foot, which can be a relatively strenuous exercise due to the extreme heat, difficult underfoot conditions and vertiginous edges.

The most accessible hiking circuits run through the so-called **Petit Tsingy**, which lies about 5km (3 miles) east of Bekopaka, and can also be accessed by pirogue from the Manambolo River Gorge. More impressive but also more challenging are the trails that run through the **Grand Tsingy** about 20km (12 miles) further north. Most trails involve crossing suspension bridges and some mild clambering. Longer outings that include abseiling down the pinnacles and harnessed climbing are offered.

MAHAJANGA

With a population nearing 250,000, **Mahajanga 20** is Madagascar's fourth-largest city and second busiest cargo port (after Toamasina, see page 59). The pretty old town incorporates an **old dhow port** lined by century-old warehouses and shops. Also worth visiting is the island's thickest and possibly oldest tree, a 700-year-old **sacred baobab** with a circumference of 20 metres (65ft) and the striking three-storey **Villa Gustave Eiffel**, built c.1890 by French engineers inspired by the metalwork of its namesake. Set within the university campus about 5km (3 miles) northeast of the city centre, the **Musée Mozea Akiba** (tel: 032-5122943; Mon–Fri 8–11am and 3–5pm, Sat–Sun 3–5pm) packs a surprising variety of fossils, local historical displays and ethnographic artefacts into its single-roomed interior.

The most tempting of several swimming beaches running north of Mahajanga is the palm-fringed **Plage du Grand Pavois**, where local kids kick around footballs on the soft white sand while traditional dhows sail past, white sails billowing in the wind. The string of unpretentious hotels and seafood restaurants that fronts Grand Pavois makes for a great sundowner or dinner spot for travellers. An ideal place to work up that thirst or appetite, **Cirque Rouge** (charge) is a spectacular 40-hectare (100-acre) amphitheatre of sedimentary cliffs

Sacred baobab

Mahajanga's sacred baobab was most likely planted by passing Arab traders 700 years ago. A *fady* forbids touching it, or digging in search of the treasure reputedly buried beneath it. Legend has it that visitors who walk around the tree seven times will be blessed on their future travels.

situated no more than 1km (0.6 miles) north of Grand Pavois. Shaded in many subtle hues of pink, white and orange, the cliffs are a product of riverine erosion and expose a horizontal sequence of ancient laterite and sandstone strata that are at their most beautiful just before dusk. A car park offers fine views over the formation, or you can walk to the main cliff base in 15 minutes, following a sandy riverbed lined with thick greenery.

ANKARAFANTSIKA NATIONAL PARK

Extending across 1,350 sq km (521 sq miles) 112km (67 miles) southeast of Mahajanga, the vast **Parc National d'Ankarafantsika** ㉑ (www.parcs-madagascar.com; 8am–4pm) supports a diverse flora comprising more than 850 plant species (90 percent of them endemic) along with plenty of lemurs and a rich birdlife. The entrance gate at **Ampijoroa** stands close to the sacred **Lac Ravelobe**, which can be explored by boat and often offers sightings of Madagascar fish-eagle, and Humblot's heron.

The best and most popular of several guided walks out of Ampijoroa is the **Circuit Grande Boucle**, which first runs through an extensive patch of dry deciduous forest notable for a unique and localised *Diplectria* tree whose outer branches grow a white snowy cover in winter to help them from dehydrating. The trail then emerges onto a grassy plateau and continues to the rim of the **Ankarokaroka Canyon**, spectacular

80-metre (260-ft) -deep sandstone gorge created by river erosion. Mammals likely to be seen in the woodland are the delightful Coquerel's sifaka and brown lemur, but the park is also the main stronghold of the mongoose lemur, a ferret-faced white-bearded frugivore listed as critically endangered. For birders, the deciduous woodland around Ampijoroa is the most reliable place countrywide for the localised Van Dam's vanga, Schlegel's asity and white-breasted mesite. The Chelonian Captive Breeding Centre (CCBC) at Ampijoroa is a breeding centre for the critically endangered ploughshare tortoise, flat-backed spider tortoise and Madagascan big-headed turtle.

THE NORTHEAST COAST

Attractions along the northeast coast range from the atmospheric Canal des Pangalanes and bustling port of Toamasina and kilometre-high forested Masoala Peninsula and idyllic offshore retreat of Île Sainte-Marie.

Canal des Pangalanes

CANAL DES PANGALANES

One of the world's longest artificial waterways, the **Canal des Pangalanes ㉒** runs south for almost 650km (404 miles) from the port of Toamasina. The earliest canals were excavated by the Imerina monarchy as the first leg of an inland transport route connecting the Toamasina to Antananarivo, but the network was vastly expanded after Madagascar became a French Colony in 1896. Though brackish in parts, it is essentially a freshwater ecosystem, flowed through by several major rivers, and it forms an important wildlife sanctuary and fishery. For tourists, gliding along the calm tree-shaded canals and open lakes that comprise this literal backwater, passing old-fashioned stick-and-rope fish traps and rustic fishing villages lined with dugout canoes, provides a fascinating glimpse into local Malagasy life away from the towns and highways.

Coming from Antananarivo 272km (168 miles) inland, the gateway to the southern Pangalanes is the village of **Manambato**, which has a lovely setting on a palm-lined white beach on the west shore of **Lac Rasoabe**. Manambato is the main boat pickup point for visitors headed deeper into the Pangalanes to stay at one of several small resorts that line the shores of **Lac Rasoamasay** and the more northerly **Lac Ampitabe**. The only genuine protected area in the Pangalanes, the 20-sq-km (7.7-sq-mile) **Réserve de Vohibola** stands on the north shore

The beach at Manambato

of Lac Ampitabe and pro-
tects one of the last two
stands of littoral rainforest
on the east coast. Managed
by the NGO Man And The
Environment (MATE) in collaboration with the local
Andranokoditra community,
this reserve is home to six
naturally occurring lemur
species, including Milne-
Edward's sifaka and red-bellied lemurs, along with 50 bird, 20
reptile and 19 amphibian species. It can be explored on three
different guided trails.

> **Salty water**
>
> Tradition holds that
> Toamasina was named by
> the visiting King Radama I,
> who had never before vis-
> ited the sea, and upon tast-
> ing its water exclaimed:
> 'Toa masina!' – literally,
> 'it's salty'.

An enjoyable and popular overnight base, the **Palmarium
Hotel** (www.palmarium.biz; charge), stands in densely-
wooded 50ha (123-acre) grounds on the west shore of Lac
Ampitabe. It supports a varied selection of free-ranging and
very habituated – and photogenic – lemurs, most of which have
been introduced and are not actually indigenous to this part of
Madagascar. A must-do for those staying overnight is the two-
hour dusk excursion to **Île au Coq**, a private reserve onto which
six aye-ayes were introduced in 2003. With its initial population
now supplemented by a couple of individuals born there, Île au
Coq is the most reliable site anywhere in Madagascar for these
most unique and fascinating of lemurs, admittedly because
they are lured to a few specific feeding sites by coconuts, so
they don't need to be actively sought.

TOAMASINA

Still sometimes referred to by its old French name
Tamatave, **Toamasina** ❷❸ is Madagascar's second-largest

city, with a population of 300,000-plus, and it accounts for three-quarters of the island's maritime trade, thanks to its deep natural harbour protected by an offshore reef, and good transport links to Antananarivo. The town centre has a relatively modern feel, though a scattering of old colonial buildings in various states of disrepair give it an underlying raffishness. **Boulevard Ratsimilaho** offers fine views across a pretty (but rather dirty) palm-lined beach to the harbour on the opposite side of Ivondro Bay. The beach here is lined with a clutter of rickety wooden beachfront bars, local eateries and fresh coconut stalls where you can watch the passing parade over a chilled beer or seafood snack. Otherwise, Toamasina offers little in the way of formal tourist attractions.

Situated about 3.5km (2 miles) offshore to the north of Toamasina, **Île aux Prunes** is a small island fringed by lovely sandy beaches and coral reefs that offer fine snorkelling. The island supports a dense cover of forest and large colonies of the Madagascar flying fox, an endangered species with a 1.25m (4ft) wingspan. Its prominent 60-metre (197ft) -high lighthouse ranks as Africa's tallest such structure, being about 1m (3ft) taller than the nearest mainland contender, at Port Said in Egypt.

Another popular day trip out of Toamasina, only 15km (9 miles) north of the city centre, the **Parc Zoologique Ivoloina** (www.parcivoloina.org; daily 9am–5pm; charge) was established in 1963 as an educational facility and refuge for wildlife confiscated by the authorities. Traversed by around 5km (3 miles) of trails, it can be explored with or without a guide, as you prefer, with the option of stopping at a stilted bird-watching hide on the lake and a small but pretty waterfall. Introduced but free-ranging populations of brown, crowned, red-bellied, great bamboo and black-and-white ruffed lemur might be seen, and the lake attracts plenty of birds including Madagascar pond heron, white-faced duck, Madagascar kingfisher and grey-headed lovebird.

FOULPOINTE

Now officially called Mahavelona, **Foulpointe** ㉔ is a is scruffy little resort village whose string of modest lodges caters mainly to weekenders from Toamasina, 60km (36 miles) further south. Ironically, its uninviting name derives from the English 'Hopeful Point', most likely coined by Captain Thomas White, an English pirate who settled there briefly c.1706. A shallow swimming beach is protected by an offshore reef, while the swanky out-of-town Azura Golf

The ruins of Fort Manda, Foulpointe

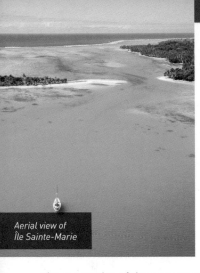

Aerial view of Île Sainte-Marie

Resort & Spa (tel: 032-0342066; www.azuragolf.mg) is home to the 9-hole **Foulpointe Golf Club**. Foulpointe also boasts a genuine historical curiosity in the form of **Fort Manda** (daily 9am–noon and 2.30–4.30pm; charge), a well-preserved and imposing circular construction built in the early 19th century by King Radama I to defend his realm against foreign naval attacks following the annexation of the east coast to Imerina.

MAHAMBO

Probably the most convincing beach resort on the northeast coastal mainland, sleepy **Mahambo** lies 30km (18 miles) north of Foulpointe at the end of a long arcing bay that offers fine conditions for swimming, surfing and snorkelling. The established focal point of tourism at Mahambo is **La Pirogue**, a mid-range hotel situated about 2km (1.2 miles) east of the RN5 along a feeder road lined with budget lodges, eateries, craft stalls and surf schools catering mainly to backpackers and a local clientele. More lived-in village than tarted-up resort, Mahambo is a refreshingly affordable and un-touristy beach destination in its own right. Logistically, it also makes for a convenient and comfortable overnight springboard for the daily boat services that run to Île Sainte-Marie from the down-at-heel estuarine port of Soanierana Ivongo to its north.

ÎLE SAINTE-MARIE

Often billed as the east coast's answer to Nosy Be, **Île Sainte-Marie** ㉕ is a 222-sq-km (86-sq-mile) island situated 7km (4 miles) offshore of the closest mainland peninsula. Officially known but seldom referred to as Nosy Boraha, the sliver-like island stretches almost 60km (36 miles) from north to south, but is nowhere significantly more than 5km (3 miles) wide, and its maximum altitude is a relatively modest 114 metres (374ft). As is the case with Nosy Be (see page 67), Sainte-Marie offers great swimming, snorkelling, diving and whale-watching opportunities, and while it lacks the

⊙ ISLAND OF PIRATES

Île Sainte-Marie's proximity to the main shipping lanes between India and Africa once made it a popular base for pirates. It started in 1685, when Adam Baldridge, an Englishman who fled Jamaica to escape charges of murder, took control of the island and imposed a tax on all ships that docked there, as well as maintaining a harem of Malagasy women he pimped to passing ship-hands. By the end of the century, the island and bay were entrenched as retreat for rogues and profiteers, among them William 'Captain' Kidd, Henry 'Long Ben' Avery (the subject of Daniel Defoe's The King of Pirates) and Olivier Levasseur (nicknamed La Buse – The Buzzard – because of the ruthless efficiency with which he executed his attacks) - so much so that one map from 1733 simply refers to Île Sainte-Marie as 'Island of Pirates'.

spectacular volcanic scenery and lemur-filled forests of its western counterpart, it compensates by being less overtly touristy and considerably more affordable. Weather permitting, daily motorboat shuttles run back and forth between the mainland riverport of Soanierana Ivongo and the island's principal town Ambodifotatra, a 30km (18-mile) crossing that takes up to 90 minutes. However, most visitors opt to fly there from Antananarivo or Toamasina, landing at **Sainte-Marie Airport** at Ankarena, about 13km (8 miles) south of Ambodifotatra.

Ambodifotatra, the island's largest settlement, stands on its southeast coast overlooking the shallow **Baie aux Forbans** (Pirate's Bay) and the two islets that punctuate it. At the south end of town, the **Colline d'Ambodifotatra** is dominated by an arched double-storey fort constructed by the French in 1753, making it the oldest extant structure on Sainte-Marie. About 100 metres/yds to its south, the neat **Eglise Notre-Dame-de-l'Assomption** is Madagascar's oldest Catholic church, built in 1857 on the site of a Jesuit mission founded 20 years earlier. A short causeway leads from the town to **Îlot Madame**, a small built-up island named after Queen Bity of Betsimisaraka, who signed a treaty ceding Sainte-Marie to France in 1750. Another bridge

Eulophiella roempleriana orchid

leads from Îlot Madame to the south shore of the bay, where the scenically located **Cimetière des Pirates** (Pirates' cemetery; (daily 8am–5pm; free), houses 30-odd tombstones marking the graves of 18th-century pirates and 19th-century missionaries.

Vohilava, on the west coast 15 minutes' drive south of Ambodifotatra, lies

> ## Orchids
>
> The largest and most beautiful of Madagascar's orchids, the epiphytic *Eulophiella roempleriana* has stunning pink, purple and white flowers clustered on a long spike. All-but-confined to the east coast of Île aux Nattes, it is easy to locate when it flowers over December and January.

at the heart of Sainte-Marie's most developed tourist strip, a 3km (2-mile) stretch of beach lined with a dozen or so hotels. All these lodges offer a wide range of marine activities: snorkelling in the shallow coral reefs of the sand cays; scuba diving alongside turtles, manta rays and the like at the 30-metres (100ft) -deep **Barracuda** and **Treasure Islands**; day visits to the east coast's utterly gorgeous and unspoilt **Baie d'Ampanihy**; or whale-watching excursions in search of the 16-metre/yd-long humpbacks that lob-tail and calve offshore during the southern winter months, most visibly over July to September. A narrow channel divides Île Sainte-Marie from the 2.8-sq-km (1.1-sq-mile) **Île aux Nattes**, whose white sandy beaches fulfil every expectation of an Indian Ocean island idyll, and are also lined with a burgeoning collection of attractive resort hotels.

MAROANTSETRA AND THE MASOALA PENINSULA

Madagascar's ultimate end-of-the-road town, **Maroantsetra** ㉖ is an isolated seaport situated at the mouth of the **Antainambalana River** as it flows into the sheltered northern end of **Antongil Bay**. Maroantsetra is connected to Soanierana Ivongo by the occasional taxi-boat and a legendarily arduous stretch of the RN5, but there is no road access from the west or north, and the overwhelming majority of visitors fly in by charter.

Only 2km (1.2 miles) offshore of Maroantsetra, the 5.2-sq-km (2-sq-mile) **Réserve Spéciale de Nosy Mangabe** (www.parcs-madagascar.com; charge) protects Antongil Bay's largest island, a lovely forested protrusion that rises to a summit of 332 metres (1090ft) above the surrounding turquoise waters. Nosy Mangabe was originally set aside as a reserve to protect an introduced population of aye-aye, and it is also home to black-and-white ruffed lemur, white-fronted lemur and a wide variety of birds, reptiles and frogs. Between July and September, several thousand humpback whales gather in Antongil Bay to breed, and they can frequently be seen breaching and lob-tailing from Nosy Mangabe.

Only 20km (12 miles) east of Maroantsetra, the 2,400 sq km (927 sq miles) **Parc National de Masoala ㉗** (www.parcs-madagascar.com; charge) is Madagascar's largest national park, and a key component of the **Rainforests of the Atsinanana Unesco World Heritage Site**. Rising from a succession of stunning uninhabited beaches to a series of tall peaks (maximum altitude 1,310 metres/4,298ft), it protects an extraordinary diversity of wooded and wetland habitats, and is an important stronghold for several localised birds, notably Madagascar serpent eagle, Madagascar red owl, pitta-like ground-roller, rufous-headed ground-roller, Bernier's vanga and helmet vanga. Other wildlife includes 15 species of lemur, the spectacular tomato frog, and the gorgeous day-flying Madagascar sunset moth, whose iridescent wings have a span of up to 10cm (4in). Masoala is accessible only by boat and is best

Rare emperor moth, Parc National de Masoala

suited to fit and adventurous travellers willing to embark on a 3–14 day hiking trip between the official national park campsite and cottage.

NOSY BE

Madagascar's most popular seaside destination, **Nosy Be** ⓪ is a lush and scenic tropical island renowned for its relaxed ambience, agreeable year-round weather, superb diving and beaches. Its evocative name translates somewhat prosaically as 'Big Island', a reference to its status as the largest component in an archipelago of partially-submerged Holocene volcanoes that rise from the clear shallow turquoise waters of Madagascar's northwestern continental shelf. Touristically, it functions as something of an island apart, serviced by its own international airport and flights from Europe, South Africa, Réunion and Mayotte – indeed, though the island is only 30 minutes by boat from the port of **Ankify**, the majority of visitors to Nosy Be never set foot on the Malagasy mainland.

HELL-VILLE

The largest town on Nosy Be and main mooring point for boats to and from Ankify, **Hell-Ville Ⓐ** stands on the island's south coast, and its name - far from reflecting any hellish qualities - is commemorative of Admiral Anne Chrétien Louis de Hell, the French Governor of Isle de Bourbon (now Réunion) whose 1939 treaty of protectorateship with Queen Tsiomeko of Boina led to the formal annexation of Nosy Be to France in 1841. An attractive town of 40,000 residents, Hell-Ville possesses an interesting colonial architectural heritage. This is particularly so on the wide **Rue Passot** (aka Cours de Hell) and **Boulevard de l'Indépendance**, which are

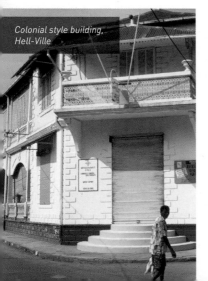

Colonial style building, Hell-Ville

lined with two- and three-storey colonial administrative buildings whose down-at-heel state only partially detracts from former pomp.

The most important cultural site in the vicinity of Hell-Ville is the **Arbre Sacré de Mahatsinjo Ⓑ** (9am–5pm; charge), a sacred banyan *Ficus religiosa* planted by Indian settlers in honour of the first visit to the island by Queen Tsiomeko of Boina and her 12,000-strong

Sakalava army back in 1837. Sprawling across hundreds of square metres, this multiple-trunked tree is draped with red-and-white cloths and the skulls and horns of zebus sacrificed there, and hosts a free-ranging population of black lemurs. The sacred site is overseen by the adjacent **Espace Zeny**, a private ethnographic museum that displays more than 100 old photographs relating to the Sakalava people, along with other cultural and historical objects. Mahatsinjo and its sacred tree stand about 3km (2 miles) from the central market, and can be reached by following the Route de l'Ouest for roughly 2km (1.2 miles), then turning left onto the sign-posted feeder road. You need to remove your shoes before visiting the site and, if wearing shorts, may be asked to wear a wraparound cloth.

BEACHES

The hub of tourist activity on Nosy Be is the idyllic string of beaches that stretches along the southwest coast, starting about 10km (6 miles) from Hell-Ville along the surfaced Route de l'Ouest. All of the beaches have shallow inclines and are protected by tall headlands, ensuring calm seas and safe swimming conditions all year round. Far and away the most developed beach, southerly **Ambatoloaka ⓒ** is lined with hotels, restaurants, cafés, handicraft boutiques, supermarkets, dive centres, tour operators, ATMs, spas, and hopeful taxi drivers and fixers. **Madirokely ⓓ** is essentially a northerly extension of Ambatoloaka – difficult to say where one beach starts and the other ends – but less developed and commercialised. A tall craggy headland separates Madirokely from **Ambondrona ⓔ**, probably the island's loveliest beach, totally hassle-free, and lined with more low-key hotels whose restaurants and pools literally spill out onto the sand. The more urbanised beach at **Dzamandzary**, separated from

Ambondrona by another impressive headland, is distinguished by its location opposite the tiny island of **Nosy Tanga**, while the more northerly and less developed beaches at **Bemoko** and **Ambaro** face the larger and taller **Nosy Sakatia**.

MONT PASSOT AND LOKOBE

Dominating the northwestern interior of Nosy Be, multiple-coned 329m (1,080ft) **Mont Passot** Ⓕ incorporates the island's second-highest peak, and is accessible by an all-weather road that passes close to eight crater lakes, ranging in size from pond-like **Lac Ambalavato** to the 1,200m/yd-wide **Lac Amparihibe** (the island's main source of piped drinking water). At the summit, a horseshoe-shaped wooden platform offers splendid views in all directions, and is perfectly positioned to

View from Mont Passot to the crater lake, Lac Amparihibe

catch the sunset. A short network of walking trails connecting the summit to the various lakes can be covered in a couple of hours. Tempting as it may look, however, fishing or swimming in the brilliant green lakes, which are believed to host the spirits of the Sakalava monarchy, is *fady*. There's also a taboo on fishing, and on harming the sacred crocodiles that have a reputation for enforcing the swimming *fady*.

The far southeast of Nosy Be is dominated by the 8-sq-km (3-sq-mile) **Réserve Naturelle Intégrale de Lokobe G** (www. parcs-madagascar.com; daily 8am–4pm; charge), which protects the island's last remaining stand of undisturbed indigenous forest. It is named after the 455 metre (1,492ft) high **Mont Lokobe**, whose volcanic slopes support the glamorous black lemur as well as the unobtrusive Hawk's sportive lemur and Claire's mouse lemur. Other wildlife includes the blue morph of panther chameleon, whose striking coloration is restricted to the population centred on Nosy Be and the nearby mainland. The park is traversed by three short walking trails across rugged terrain that requires some fitness and agility. A tamer and more contrived alternative to Lokobe, nearby **Lemuria Land** (www.lemurialand.com; daily 8am–5pm; charge) is a glorified private zoo aimed squarely at the beach package holiday market.

OTHER ISLANDS

Magnificent **Nosy Komba H** (Island of Lemurs) is distinguished by its classic volcanic profile of steep slopes swathed in a multihued green blanket of rainforest and tall bamboo. A popular destination for boat excursions from Nosy Be, just 3km (1.8 miles) to its north, it can also be visited directly from mainland Ankify, and all three are connected by a regular public ferry service. **Ampangorina** (charge),

Nosy Iranja

the island's largest settlement, is renowned for its profusion of black lemurs, which frequently leap on visitors in hope of food. More challenging but thoroughly rewarding excursion is the steep but scenic hike to **Antagnianaomby**, the highest point on the island at 622 metres (2,041ft). A local *fady* means that this can only be undertaken on Mondays and Saturdays, and a traditional *lambahoany* (printed cotton cloth sarong) must be worn by climbers.

Situated about 8km (5 miles) west of Nosy Komba, **Parc National Marin de Nosy Tanikely** ❶ (www.parcs-madagascar. com; daily 8am–4pm daily) was created in 2011 to protect the tiny island for which it is named, as well as the surrounding sea, whose multi-coloured coral reefs form one of Madagascar's most popular and finest diving and snorkelling sites. Another excellent snorkelling site, mangrove-lined **Nosy Sakatia** ❿ (Island of Forbidden Love), lies little more than 1km (0.6 miles) offshore of the west coast of Nosy Be. Somewhat more remote, situated about 35km (21 miles) southwest of Nosy Be, **Nosy Iranja** ⓚ – actually two forested islets linked by a 1km (0.6-mile) -long sandbar – is an important breeding site for marine turtles and also offers good snorkelling. More remote still, **Nosy Tsarabanjina** ⓛ, an idyllic islet in the Mitsio Archipelago northeast of Nosy Be, now houses the super-luxurious and equally pricey Constance Tsarabanjina, a five-star destination accessible only by charter flight from Nosy Be.

THE FAR NORTH

Rising from the world's second-largest natural bay, the unspoilt beaches, montane forests and jagged tsingy of the Diana Region - the most northerly of Madagascar's 22 administrative regions - can be explored from the relaxed port city of Diego Suarez.

DIEGO SUAREZ

Among the most agreeable of Malagasy towns, **Diego Suarez** ㉙ occupies a wide, tall peninsula that protrudes into the eponymous 20km- (12-mile) -long bay. It is most likely named after Diogo Soares de Albergaria, a Portuguese adventurer whose acts of piracy led to a warrant for his arrest being issued by Governor da Gama of Goa in 1540. The modern town is essentially a French colonial creation, founded after the first Franco-Malagasy War of 1883–5. It was an important naval base in World War II, captured and occupied by the British in May 1942 in order to prevent the pro-Nazi Régime de Vichy from signing a treaty allowing it to be used by Japanese warships and submarines. Now supporting a population of 120,000, Madagascar's most northerly large town is officially known as Antsiranana ('Place of the Port'), but still almost ubiquitously referred to as Diego by locals and foreigners alike.

A good place to start a walking tour, **Place Foch** is a large tree-shaded central square surrounded by old colonial administrative buildings and graced by a bust of Philibert Tsiranana. Running northward, **Rue Colbert** was laid out in the 1890s and remains the main commercial road, lined with half-a-dozen cafés and restaurants, as well as a good selection of supermarkets and craft boutiques, and the **Alliance Française** (housed in a prefabricated metal structure designed by the Eiffel Workshop and erected in 1925 to replace the original wooden market). At the north end of Rue Colbert, historic Rue Richelieu is flanked by the old **Tribunal**, built in 1908, and the attractive two-storey **La Résidence**, built to replace the original Hôtel du Gouvernement in 1892. Rue Richelieu terminates at **Place Joffre**, a small circular clifftop lookout that once served as the receiving point for optical telegraph signals from Cap d'Ambre, and is now lined with benches from where you can watch the harbour lights as the sun sets over the western bay.

About 1km (0.6 miles) south of the town centre, a pair of war cemeteries are the final resting place of the casualties associated with the 1942 Allied naval assault on Diego Suarez. The **Diego Suarez Military Cemetery** on Boulevard Duplex contains the tombs of 921 French, other Europeans and Malagasy killed in action between the 1890s and 1960s, but is dominated by soldiers who fought for Vichy France in 1942. A block east of this, the well-tended **Diego Suarez War Cemetery** (daily 8am–4pm) contains the graves of 314 Commonwealth soldiers, sailors and airmen who died in action here over 1942–4, as well as one Belgian fatality.

Continue for another 2km (1.2km) south along Boulevard Duplex, past the prominent junction with the RN6, and you'll emerge on a cliff offering lovely views to **Nosy Lonjo**, the small but steep 120-metre (393ft) -high island depicted on the back of the 100 ariary banknote, and also known as Pain de Sucre (Sugarloaf) on account of its rather tenuous resemblance to the much larger Rio de Janeiro landmark. Nosy Lonjo means 'Island of Strength', in reference to a powerful sacred stone used for rituals invoking the ancestral spirits. The forested island remains uninhabited and it is *fady* to step ashore for secular reasons – indeed, it is said than anybody who does so will be destined to die soon afterwards.

MONTAGNE DES FRANÇAIS

Rising to 425 metres (1,395ft) 5km (3 miles) immediately southeast of central Diego, tsingy-capped **Montagne des Français** is an important watershed and biodiversity hotspot. The massif has a long history of military occupation. In 1828, the Imerina monarchy built a fort there to repel naval attempts to occupy the bay below. In the wake of the French protectorateship treaty of 1885, the imposing colonial **Fort d'Anosiravo** was constructed on the northern summit, using rocks carried up along a funicular railway. During World War II, the mountain was a pivotal battleground in the British and Commonwealth defeat of the Vichy government in May 1942.

Montagne des Français is now the focal point of the **Circuit d'Anosiravo** (7am–4pm), a community-based project comprising a guided 2.5-hour, 5km (3-mile) circular nature trail and optional 1km (0.6-mile) historical extension. Best undertaken in the cool of the morning, this superb trail offers fantastic views over the Baie des Français to Nosy Lonjo. Look out for the spectacular Suarez baobab *Adansonia suarezensis*, a highly localised tree distinguished from other members of the genus by its smooth red-brown bark, cylindrical trunk and neat crown of horizontal

Adansonia suarezensis (Suarez baobab)

Rules of the trail

It is *fady* to urinate on the Montagne des Français, so make sure you visit a toilet before you hike the Circuit d'Anosiravo. Carry drinking water, as it can get very hot on the exposed lower slopes.

branches. Wildlife includes crowned lemur, giant day gecko, and 60 bird species. The highlight of the trail is the steep historic extension, which climbs through the jagged tsingy to the significant remains of Fort d'Anosiravo via the cleft formerly traversed by the funicular railway.

RAMENA AND THE EMERALD SEA

The most popular beach destination in the vicinity of Diego Suarez, **Ramena** is a compact village situated on the inner (eastern) shore of the peninsula that separates the Baie des Français from the open sea. Geared more towards Diego weekenders than foreign tourists, it has a fine swimming beach, and a host of welcoming and unpretentious seafood restaurants and bars line the beach either side of the central jetty. It is also the springboard for day excursions to **La Mer d'Emeraude 30**, a beautiful, pale turquoise lagoon that offers superb swimming conditions and great snorkelling in the calm weather that usually prevails between December and April. Half-day trips, including snorkelling gear and lunch, can be arranged through any operator or hotel in the area.

PARC NATIONAL DE LA MONTAGNE D'AMBRE

Rising to 1,477 metres (4,845ft) southwest of Diego Suarez, Montagne d'Ambre is an ancient volcanic mountain named after a type of tree resin believed locally to possess curative qualities. Its footslopes are an important centre of agriculture, but since 1958 the rainforest-swathed upper slopes have been protected in the 182-sq-km (70-sq-mile) **Parc National de la Montagne d'Ambre** ③ (www.parcs-madagascar.com; daily 8am–4pm; charge). The gateway to the park is the leafy colonial-style village of **Joffreville**, which was founded in 1902 as a retreat for military personnel stationed at Diego Suarez, 45 minutes away by road (see page 73). From the ticket office 3km (2 miles) uphill of Joffreville, a 20km (12-mile) trail network runs through liana-draped 40-metre (131ft) -high rainforest, past a scattering of emerald-green crater lakes and pretty waterfalls. Several guided hiking variations are available: the shorter options are more rewarding for wildlife, because they give you more time to stop and search for smaller species, but the longer trails have more scenic variety.

Crater lake, Parc National de la Montagne d'Ambre

Rock Thrush,
Montagne d'Ambre

Isolated from other similar habitats, the forests of the Montagne d'Ambre are renowned for their floral variety. More than 1,000 plant species have been recorded here, among them several flowering orchids, and the epiphytic bird's-nest fern with its 3-metre (10ft) -long fronds. The forest also boasts an extraordinary level of endemism. Of 14 recorded chameleon species, a full nine occur nowhere else in the world. Montagne d'Ambre also supports the world's greatest diversity of leaf-tailed geckos (see page 38), and 75 bird species including Madagascar crested ibis, pitta-like ground-roller, Madagascar cuckoo-roller, greater vasa parrot, white-throated oxylabes, and Amber Mountain rock thrush (whose entire global population is confined to this one single forest block). Mammals are less conspicuous, but you can expect to see crowned lemur and Sanford's brown lemur, and the fossa is quite often encountered on afternoon walks during the main breeding season on November.

SOUTH OF DIEGO

Justifiably one of the busiest tourist attractions in this part of Madagascar, **Site Communautaire des Tsingy Rouges** ❸❷ (7am–5pm; charge) stands about 17km (10 miles) east of

the RN6 along a dirt road that's signposted about 40km (25 miles) south of Diego Suarez. Unlike the larger, sharper and harder black tsingy mountains found elsewhere in northern Madagascar, this site protects an otherworldly landscape of curvaceous and crumbly laterite chimneys that typically stand up to 5 metres (16ft) high and possess a texture reminiscent of enlarged coral or lung tissue. The best time to be there is late afternoon or early morning, when the soft light enhances the natural reddish hues of the ferruginous clay, and temperatures tend to be more tolerable.

The most accessible of Madagascar's major tsingy formations, the **Réserve Spéciale d'Ankarana** ❸❸ (www.parcs-madagascar.com; daily 7.30am–4pm; charge) extends across an area of 182 sq km (70 sq miles) immediately west of the

Tsingy formations, Réserve Spéciale d'Ankarana

RN6 at Mahamasina, 105km (63 miles) south of Diego Suarez. Ankarana's dominant feature is the immense eponymous limestone formation, which rises from a low-lying eastern base to a 25km (15 mile) long western wall that peaks at 206 metres (676ft). The massif incorporates around 100km (60 miles) of mapped passages, the longest cave network in Madagascar, possibly the whole of Africa. The reserve is home to 330 plant, 11 lemur, 96 bird, 44 reptile and 16 amphibian species.

◎ TSINGY

A surreal and forbidding landscape characteristic of northern Madagascar, Tsingy – which translates as 'Place you cannot walk barefoot' – is a karstic formation whose deeply-incised clusters or spines of steep, serrated rock needles are often likened to stone forests. These jagged natural sculptures are carved into sedimentary limestone plateaux that formed in a shallow marine habitat in the Jurassic period, but were subsequently subjected to tectonic uplift, which not only raised them above sea level, but also caused them to develop a grid of vertical and horizontal cracks. Limestone being partially soluble, these linear cracks were then eroded by mildly acid rainwater into larger fissures that eventually exposed the strange striated and pinnacled formations we see today. Madagascar's largest block of tsingy is found in the remote Parc National des Tsingy de Bemaraha, but several smaller formations also exist, with those in Ankarana being the most accessible, since they stand alongside the RN6 between Nosy Be and Diego Suarez.

Several guided day-walks can be arranged at the main entrance in **Mahamasina**. The shortest circuit, 3km (1.8 miles) in either direction, leads to the **Tsingy Meva** and the **Grottes des Chauves-Souris**, which as its name suggests is home to up to 50,000 bats. Another short circuit, 5km (miles) in either direction, leads to the **Tsingy Ravy** and the **Perte des Rivières**, a massive circular sinkhole

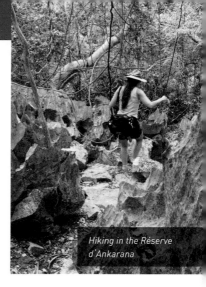

Hiking in the Réserve d'Ankarana

where two rivers vanish underground. The more demanding and rewarding **Moyen Circuit**, running for 10km (6 miles) in either direction, is a 20km (12-mile) round trip into the **Grandes Tsingy**, crossing a large ravine via a pair of suspension bridges spanning 22 metres (72ft) and 6 metres (20ft). Slightly longer, at 11km (7 miles) in either direction (allow nine hours for the round trip), is the **Grand Circuit**, which also takes you to the small but beautiful **Lac Vert**, set in the base of a wooded ravine.

Situated just outside Ankarana's southwestern border, the **Iharana Massif**, a large isolated tsingy outcrop that rises to 123 metres (403ft) above the pretty lake at its northern base, is managed as a private reserve by **Iharana Bush Camp** in collaboration with the local Antsaravibe community, and can be traversed on an excellent three-hour guided walking trail, complete with rope ladders and small bridges across the tsingy peaks.

Fossa in the wild

WHAT TO DO

Madagascar is very much a country for outdoor enthusiasts, whether of a sedentary or more active disposition. Beach destinations such as Nosy Be and Île Sainte-Marie are tailor-made for those who idea of activity entails sauntering languidly between swimming pool, beach and terrace restaurant, but the dazzling offshore reefs and lush national parks of the interior offer superb opportunities for wildlife watching, hiking, rafting and other more energetic pursuits.

SPORTS AND OUTDOOR ACTIVITIES

WILDLIFE WATCHING

The main wildlife attraction in Madagascar is its 100-plus species of lemur, many of which have a very localised distribution and are listed as critically endangered. Lemur viewing isn't strongly seasonal but some smaller species hibernate and are more difficult to see in midwinter. Baby lemurs start to appear in November, adding greatly to the excitement of an encounter. October to November is when the fossa, the island's largest carnivore, goes into breeding mode and tends to be most conspicuous.

Unlike mainland Africa, wildlife-watching is almost invariably undertaken on foot, partly because the island lacks for potentially dangerous large mammals, but more so because the nature of the terrain protected in the network of 50-plus national parks, special reserves and other conservation areas managed by **Madagascar National Parks** (MNP; www.parcs-madagascar.com) is typically thickly-forested, or prohibitively mountainous, or both. Most of these reserves are open to tourists, but some are considerably more accessible and have better amenities than others. In terms of ready accessibility and overall wildlife-viewing, the most popular and worthwhile MNP destinations for short-term visitors are probably **Andasibe-Mantadia**, **Ranomafana**, **Ankarana**, **Isalo** and **Montagne d'Ambre**.

It is forbidden to enter any MNP property without an official guide, to walk in it after dark (night walks are now conducted outside park boundaries), or to build lodges inside it. All national parks charge a daily entrance fee, as well as fixed guide-fees that are determined in conjunction with the local guides association, and often depend on the length of walk and degree of guiding skill. Almost without exception, all charges

Indri lemur with cub

are clearly itemised at the park's ticket office, and arrangements can be made on the spot.

In addition, Madagascar hosts a number of other government-run, community-managed or private conservation areas, most notably the admirable community-run **Réserve d'Anja** (famed for its ring-railed lemurs) and popular **Réserve de Berenty** (a private initiative set on a sisal plantation). In most cases, these operate a similar basis to MNP properties, charging entrance as well as guide fees, but rates tend to be lower and timings more flexible.

Depending to some extent on seasonal factors, which reserve you are visit, and how far you want to walk, it is advisable to wear solid walking shoes or hiking boots on all walks and hikes, and to carry waterproof gear, drinking water, a snack and possibly a walking stick.

BIRDING

Madagascar ranks among the world's most alluring ornithological destinations thanks to an unusually high level of endemicity. The national checklist of 290 bird species embraces at least four families, 36 genera and 105 species found nowhere else in the world, along with another two families and 20 species shared only with the islands of the Comoros or Seychelles. The best time of year for birding is October and November, when several elusive species of the rainforest interior go into breeding mode and are thus more easily located by call. The onset of the rains in December reduces visibility and mobility.

The moist rainforests that cover much of eastern and northern Madagascar are most rewarding habitat in terms of avian diversity. A good location to look for endemic forest birds is the **Parc National Andasibe-Mantadia**,

Crested Coua bird

which hosts all four of the forest-associated ground-rollers, has plenty of experienced local guides, and forms a popular goal for a one- or two-night excursion from Antananarivo. Equally worthwhile is the **Parc National de Ranomafana**, which hosts a similar range of species to Mantadia. Even more rewarding, but a lot less accessible, is the vast **Parc National de Masoala**, which also forms a stronghold for the iconic helmet vanga, the highly localised Bernier's vanga and the distinctive red-breasted coua.

Almost as rewarding to visiting birdwatchers are the arid succulent-dominated spiny forests protected in several reserves near **Fort Dauphin** and **Toliara**. This area is the stronghold for several localised dry-country endemics, including the magnificent 60cm (2ft) giant coua (*Coua gigas*) and quirky long-tailed ground-roller (*Uratelornis chimaera*).

HIKING

Several of Madagascar's more remote and mountainous national parks and other conservation areas offer great scope for challenging but scenically thrilling day and multi-day hikes. The reserves that hold the most appeal to dedicated hikers include **Andringitra**, **Masoala** and **Tsingy**

de Bemaraha. As with wildlife-watching, hikers must be accompanied by a local guide, which can be arranged on the spot. Underfoot conditions for hiking are best from May to October.

Momotrek (tel: 032-4418790; www.isalo-trek.com) is specialist hiking company that arranges day and multi-day treks in **Parc National d'Isalo**. These include a five-day, four-night portered camping excursion that starts at Andriamanara in the park's little-visited north, then heads back to Ranohira in a succession of manageable legs (the longest day is 13km/8 miles).

SNORKELLING AND DIVING

The reefs and wrecks off the coast off Madagascar offer some superb opportunities for snorkelling and diving. The

⊙ PAYS ZAFIMANIRY

The mist-swept forested highlands southeast of Ambositra are home to the Zafimaniry people, whose traditional woodcraft skills and knowledge form the only Madagascan inclusion on Unesco's Intangible Cultural Heritage List. The Zafimaniry build their houses entirely from timber, without using nails, and they decorate the exterior, as well as all furniture therein, with geometric patterns that reflect their ancient Indonesian heritage as well as a more recent Arab influence. They are also one of the last Malagasy ethnic groups to still erect stone obelisks to commemorate their ancestors. Hikes into the Pays Zafimaniry can be arranged through Sous le Soleil de Mada (tel: 033-0734414; http://sous lesoleildemada.monsite-orange.fr).

*Green sea turtle,
Nosy Tanikely*

country's premier destination for underwater activities is **Nosy Be** and surrounding islands such as **Nosy Tanikely**, **Nosy Sakatia**, **Nosy Iranja** and **Nosy Tsarabanjina**. In addition to a dazzlingly kaleidoscopic menagerie of reef-dwellers such as surgeonfish, damselfish, butterfly fish, clownfish, parrotfish and devil's firefish, these sites offer a good chance of encountering marine turtles and other giants of the deep such as whale shark. Diving and snorkelling is quite good throughout the year but visibility tends to be best and water calmest over August to October, when storms are few and far between, and there's less sediment is brought down by rivers.

Recommended operators in Nosy Be are Scuba Nosy Be (Ambondrona Beach, tel 032-0796158, www.scubanosybe. com), which runs PADI, SSI and CMAS certified dives to all nearby islands, as well as several wreck sites, and Mada Scuba (Ambatoloaka Beach, tel: 032-2175768, www.mada-scuba. com), which offers reliable scuba diving and snorkelling trips to most sites in the vicinity.

Another good diving site is **Île Sainte-Marie**, where leading operators include Bora Dive & Research (tel: 032-0709090, www.facebook.com/BoraDiveResearch), a dive and oceanographic research centre that offers PADI courses,

dives and a variety of other marine activities out of the affili-
ated Princess Bora Lodge & Spa, and the long-serving dive
shop Lémurien Palmé (tel: 020-5704015, www.lemurien-
palme.com), which is based in Ambodifotatra and offers
scuba dives, snorkelling excursion and seasonal whale-
watching trips.

At the resort of **Ifaty-Mangily** north of Toliara, several
operators offer all-inclusive snorkelling and diving trips to the
offshore Massif des Roses and Ankaranjelita, which support a
great diversity of fish, with the latter being quieter human-wise
and more productive fish-wise, but also more xpensive to visit
as it is further away. Recommendations are Mangily Scuba (tel:
034-6478176; www.ifatyscuba.com) and Atimoo Plongée (tel:
034-0252917; www.atimoo.com).

*Breaching humpback whale,
Île Sainte-Marie*

WHALE- AND DOLPHIN-WATCHING

The waters off Madagascar are home to 30-plus species of cetaceans (whales and dolphins) as well as the seaweed-guzzling manatee-like dugong. The most conspicuous aquatic mammal off Nosy Be - often seen on boat trips to the reefs and other islands - is the spinner dolphin (*Stenella longirostris*), which regularly moves in schools of several hundred individuals and is named for its spectacular habit of rotating longitudinally as it leaps through the air. One of its most renowned marine spectacles is the several thousand humpback whale Megaptera novaeangliae that gather to breed over July and September in **Antongil Bay**, where they are most easily seen from the **Réserve Spéciale de Nosy Mangabe**. Seasonal whale watching excursions, with activity peaking over the northerly

⊙ A GENTLE GIANT

Nosy be is considered to be something of a hotspot for underwater sightings of the whale shark *Rhincodon typus*, which is the world's largest fish, and easily distinguished by the combination of immense bulk, wide mouth and spotted skin pattern. An adult typically attains a length of 12 metres (40ft) and weighs up to 35 tonnes, but can be 50 percent larger than that. Despite its intimidating size, the whale shark is a filter-feeder whose main diet is plankton and other microscopic organisms, and it is essentially harmless to humans (though snorkellers or divers who get too close to its powerful tail fins risk being swiped). An estimated global numerical decline of at least 60 percent since the turn of the millennium, mainly as a result of overfishing, led to the whale shark being IUCN-listed as endangered in 2016.

migration that takes place along the west coast from July to September, are offered by dive and tour operators in most other coastal resorts.

HORSEBACK EXCURSIONS

Horseback trips close to Antananarivo can be undertaken at the Ferme Equestre du Rova (tel: 032 -0703904; www.cheval-madagascar.com), which is based on the shore of

Horse riding, Nosy Be

Lake Andranotapahina, to the northwest of the city centre. On the popular island of Nosy Be, Ranch Ambaro (Route du Nord; tel: 032-4369178; http://ambaroranchnosybe.blogspot.co.za) offers family-friendly horseback excursions on the beaches and slopes of the west coast. Another place that offers horseback trips is Vakona Forest Lodge's Les Ecuries de Falierada (www.hotelvakona.com; tel: 033-6697471), a stable offering trips ranging from 30 minutes to two hours in duration near Parc National Andisibe-Mantadia.

GOLFING

Opportunities for golfing in Madagascar are rather limited. The country's only 18-hole course is the International Golf Club du Rova (tel: 020-2201190), which was established on the northern outskirts of Antananarivo back in the colonial era and accepts day members. On the east coast north of Toamasina, Foulpointe Golf

Club is a 9-hole beachfront course set in the swanky Azura Golf Resort & Spa (tel: 032-0342066; www.azuragolf.mg). It is open to day visitors, caddies are available, and clubs can be rented.

KAYAKING AND BOATING

Morondava's long-serving Remote River Expeditions (tel: 020-9552347, www.remoterivers.com), based at the perennially popular Chez Maggie Hotel, is the acknowledged specialist when it comes to arranging boat trips on the **Tsiribihina**, **Manambolo** and other rivers in western Madagascar.

Rafting is available in two other more accessible national parks. In **Ranomafana**, Varibolo Resto (tel: 034-9082303; www.varibolo.com; 7am–8pm) operates expertly guided kayaking trips on the **Namorona** (aka Andriamamovoka) **River**,

Boat trip on the Manambolo River

departing at 9am daily and taking around three hours. In Andisibe-Mantadia, the small Parc Voi MMA; tel: 034-1570496; daily 7am–4pm) offers self-paddled or guided kayak trips upstream along the **Analamazaotra River** into the forest, or downstream to its confluence with the Vohitra a short distance east of Andasibe Railway Station.

Rare wood

When purchasing wood products, ensure they are not made out of rare and endangered species such as rosewood (also known as *palissandre*), which is important traditionally but has been harvested at an ecologically destructive rate in recent years.

SURFING AND KITESURFING

The top surf school in **Fort Dauphin**, Born Naked (Plage d'Ankoba, tel: 032-6976162, www.surfbornnaked.com) also offers boards for hire and full packages aimed at surf enthusiasts. Summer Session Surfing (tel: 033-7665996, www.facebook.com/SummerSessionSurfingSchool/) has surfboards for hire and surfing lessons are offered on lovely Mahambo Beach north of **Toamasina**. Near **Diego Suarez**, Kitesurf Madagascar (tel. 032-4498554, www.kitesurfmadagascar.com) is based on the windswept beach at Baie de Sakalava, the country's best bay for this increasingly popular sport.

SHOPPING

Madagascar offers some great opportunities for craft and souvenir shopping. Popular items with foodies include the world's finest vanilla, sold in clumps of dried beans that look like irregularly-shaped liquorice sticks, and other home-grown products such as cloves, green or black pepper, and coffee. Fragrant massage oils are made from the ylang-ylang flower and other local products, and it's worth checking your home country's duty-free allowances to bring back a couple of bottles of local rum, which might be infused with anything from ginger or vanilla to lemons and oranges.

Local **handicrafts** are also popular with souvenir shoppers. These include scarves and other garments woven from traditionally-manufactured wild silk, patch-worked cloth squares known as lamba, and a wide variety of metalwork, basketry, woodcarving and zebu horn and leather goods. The country's finest craftsmen are probably the **Zafimaniry** woodworkers of **Fianarantsoa**, whose intricate work forms the only Madagascan inclusion on the Unesco Intangible Cultural Heritage List.

Most towns have small markets or boutique selling handicrafts, none as impressive or varied as the 100-stall-strong **Marché Artisanal de la Digue**, which lies alongside the main road between Antananarivo and Ivato International Airport. In many cases, however, it is more supportive of local communities and craftsmen to buy their products from individuals or local markets close to the source.

ENTERTAINMENT

Madagascar doesn't exactly have a thumping nightlife or arts scene, but most towns and tourist resorts are equipped with some characterful little bars and bistros. In certain beach resorts, particularly on Nosy Be, prostitution is a conspicuous facet of many tourist-oriented bars. The country's best-known and most tourist-friendly nightclub is Antananarivo's Kudeta Urban Club (Rue Ranaivo Junes, tel: 020-2261140, www.lapasoa.com/kudeta-urban-club), which is based in the Carlton Hotel.

ACTIVITIES FOR CHILDREN

The Malagasy people generally adore children and most hotels will gladly accommodate them. Children are also offered discounts on admission fees to most places of interest. That said, away from Nosy Be and a handful of other dedicated beach resorts, the challenges of travel in Madagascar (and the unpackaged nature of its main attractions) are likely to be even more daunting with young or easily bored children in tow. Very few hotels offer formal baby-sitting services.

Ambatoloaka beach, Nosy Be

FESTIVALS AND EVENTS

Madagascar has a rather limited bouquet of festivals, but the following will be of interest to some visitors:

Third week of May The Zegny'Zo Arts Festival in Diego Suarez is a street festival curated in collaboration with the Alliance Française. Its attractions including dancing, puppetry, drama, street painting, music, circus-acts and parades.

Pentecost – May or June The week-long Donia Festival on Nosy Be offers a great opportunity to see traditional and contemporary musicians from Madagascar and elsewhere in Africa and the Indian Ocean.

Mid-June Antananarivo's Carnaval de Madagascar, held over three days during the build up to the Fête de l'Indépendance, hosts musical and other traditional artists from all over the Indian Ocean region.

26 June Fête de l'Indépendance (Independence Day) is still vigorously celebrated all over Madagascar six decades after the event. The biggest celebrations are in Antananarivo, where much of the city centre closes down for several days, but there's a party atmosphere, with live music and the like, in most large towns.

October Established in 1988 and still going strong, Madajazzcar in Antananarivo is held over two weeks and features a combination of home-grown jazz musicians and their counterparts from the US, Europe, Asia, mainland Africa and the nearby islands of Mauritius and Réunion.

EATING OUT

The capital Antananarivo offers visitors a good range of international restaurants catering mainly to the expatriates and wealth locals. These tend to be dominated by French and to a lesser extent Italian cuisine, but you will also find Indian, Chinese, Southeast Asian, Lebanese and other African cuisines represented. There are also fast-food chains serving burgers, pizzas, fried chicken and the like. Mains tend to cost a bit more in Antananarivo than elsewhere in the country, but it is cheap by international standards so there is no need to pay a small fortune to eat well.

Elsewhere, the choices tend to be more limited. Restaurants can be found in the smallest of towns, but most are unpretentious establishments that serve a simple (but often very tasty) *plat du jour* – most likely, chicken or beef stew with rice – for a couple of euros to a predominantly Malagasy clientele.

Almost all tourist hotels and a few restaurants in most larger towns and established resorts serve up a more sophisticated and varied (but after a while rather predictable) menu of French-Malagasy

Traditional prawn curry

grilled and stewed meat and fish dishes, along with pizzas, burgers and sandwiches, catering to western palates.
Accompaniments invariably include rice, but most restaurants
also offer the choice of pommes frites, sautéed potatoes or
boiled vegetables (often swaddled in butter).

Seafood is well represented, especially on the coast, where
fresh whole line-fish, tuna steak, calamari and prawns are
usually served grilled or fried with a simple lemon, ginger or
coconut sauce.

Inland, the most popular meat is beef, which in Madagascar
is practically synonymous with zebu, a form of humped cattle introduced to the island by African settlers circa AD 1000
and later went feral, only to be re-domesticated during the
16th-century reign of King Ralambo. Usually served grilled in
the form of kebabs or a steak (often with Malagasy green pep-
percorn sauce), zebu meat tends to be far healthier than cattle meat elsewhere, because most of the island's meat comes
from more-or-less free-ranging herds.

Pork is also popular outside of Muslim areas (or other
coastal areas where pig meat is *fady*) but be alert to the fact
that the Malagasy tend to enjoy and serve far fattier cuts than
most westerners would ideally opt for. Poultry is also represented on all hotel menus, and many smarter establishments
supplement the usual chicken dishes with French specialities
such as duck and rabbit.

Menus in Madagascar tend to focus strongly on red meat,
fish and poultry, but vegetarians are unlikely to feel too
excluded, as most place have a few suitable choices. That
said, salads or other dishes listed in the vegetarian section
do often include meaty elements, so it pays to check the small
print carefully, and to interrogate the waiter when in doubt.
Vegans are seldom catered for actively, and may find it difficult

to establish what if any animal products (eggs, milk, fat) were used in the creation of a vegetarian dish.

LOCAL CUISINE

Rice is not merely the main Malagasy staple, but the very foundation of the national cuisine. The most important of several crops thought to have been shipped to the island by its original Indonesian settlers (the others include bananas, ginger and sugarcane), rice is now grown in paddies all over Madagascar, which ranks as the world's largest non-Asian producer, and is claimed to be second only to Vietnam in terms of per capita annual consumption. This is because rice forms the basis of all three main meals in most Malagasy households, a convention that has been little altered by decades of French colonialism

Malagasy street food

or – despite the growing popularity of pizza among the urban middle classes – subsequent exposure to a variety of international cuisines.

Known locally as *vary*, rice is commonly eaten for breakfast in the form of *vary sosoa*, a runny gruel-like porridge eaten plain or with a meaty sauce, or *vary aminanana*, a rice porridge cooked together with rice, meat and chopped greens. For the more sweet of tooth, *mofo gasy* (literally Malagasy bread) is a grilled circular patty of sugary rice-flour dough that rather resembles a donut and goes well with coffee or tea. Breakfast dishes not based on rice include *misao* (noodles stir-fried with chopped vegetables and meat) and *soupe chinoise* (a thin noodle soup), both of which were introduced in the early 20th century by Chinese labourers recruited to construct the railway

Mofo anana (watercress bread)

line between Antananarivo and Toamasina. Fresh baguettes and egg dishes such as omelette are also often eaten at breakfast, but generally only in hotels, smarter cafés and other establishments catering to western palates.

Lunch (the main meal in Madagascar) and dinner usually consist of boiled rice served with a meat- or vegetable-based accompaniment (known generically as *laoka*). Best

Traditional Malagasy dish of cassava, pork and rice

known among these is the national dish *romazava*, a gingery stew made from beef and vegetables (in particular a spicy leaf called *bredy mafana*). Other popular traditional accompaniments include *ravitoto* (fried meat stewed with cassava leaves and coconut milk), *voanjobory* (cubed meat and groundnuts in a garlicky tomato sauce), *vorivorinkena* (tripe and pork stew), *varanga* (shredded roast beef) and *akoho sy oanio* (chicken in a gingery coconut sauce). In practice, many local eateries in Madagascar just serve a generic tomato-based chicken, fish and/or beef stew alongside the customary mound of rice, so you generally need to visit a restaurant specialising in local cuisine to try the dishes named above.

If a stew is too bland for your taste, it can be spiced up – with caution – by adding a small teaspoon of a local condiment such as *saky* (a fiery chilli and ginger paste) or *achard* (a South Indian-style pickled mango and lemon relish).

DRINKS

Tap water is not always safe to drink but still mineral water (and to a lesser extent sparkling) is widely available. Many restaurants sell delicious freshly-squeezed or blended fruit juices, known as *jus naturel*, though sugar is almost always added unless you specify otherwise. Unusual fruit juices include those made from tamarind and baobab fruits. The usual international fizzy soft drinks are ubiquitous. A refreshing, healthy and inexpensive alternative, especially along the coast, is green coconut milk, which is sold by street vendors

⊘ VANILLA

Madagascar vies with Indonesia as the world's largest producer of vanilla, a labour-intensive crop that comprises the hand-pollinated and cured seedpods of the Mexican climbing orchid *Vanilla planifolia*, introduced by plantation owners in the late 19th century. Within Madagascar, vanilla production is focussed on coastal parts of Sava Region, whose climate is ideal for this temperamental plant. Typically, Madagascar produces up to 4,000 tonnes of vanilla annually, twice as much as Indonesia, and around 40 percent of the global yield. However, successive cyclones in 2016 and 2017 devastated production to such an extent that Indonesia's yield overtook Madagascar's for the first time. The global shortage caused the international vanilla price to climb from US$100/kg in 2015 to more than US$600/kg in 2017, making it the world's second most expensive spice after saffron. This price hike has yet to trickle down to the beleaguered smallholders who grow most of Madagascar's vanilla and receive as little as US$8/kg for their hard labour.

Vanilla pods

who will decapitate the green coconut to create a natural cup from which the juice can be sipped.

Not content with eating rice three times daily, the Malagasy also enjoy drinking it in the form of *ranovola* (also known as *ranonapango*), a tea-like concoction made by hot boiling water to the burnt rice stuck on the inside of a cooking pot. It tastes rather odd, but health-wise it has the advantage over tap water of having been boiled. Ordinary and herbal teas are also widely drunk in Madagascar, often flavoured with spices such as vanilla and ginger. The rather stew-like Malagasy-style coffee served in local eateries is an acquired taste, but larger towns usually have a few proper cafés whose coffee is geared more towards international palates.

Practically synonymous with beer in Madagascar, Three Horses (THB) is an inexpensive medium-strong (5.4 percent alcohol) pale pilsner brewed by Star Breweries at Antsirabe since 1958, and

Bottles of fruit-flavoured rum

now also produced at a second brewery in Diego Suarez catering mainly to the northern part of the island. Star Breweries also produces the stronger THB Special (6.2 percent) and a very light shandy called THB Fresh. Wine is produced at several small vineyards in the highlands around Fianarantsoa, and can be bought in most supermarkets. In most case, the quality pales by comparison to bottles imported from France and South Africa, which cost about twice as much as local produce.

Appropriately for a former pirate refuge, Madagascar is renowned for its excellent rum. A popular local speciality is *rhum arrangé*, which is basically a bottle of rum wherein a combination of tropical ingredients (most commonly ginger, vanilla, cinnamon and/or various fruits) have been left to soak to make a tasty aperitif or nightcap. Illegal home-brewed palm wine (*trembo*) and sugar cane spirits (*betsabetsa*) are also available but tend to be treacherously strong. It is traditional to throw the first capful of bottle of rum or other spirits into northeast corner of the room as an offering to the ancestral sprits.

Practically all restaurants in Madagascar are licensed (and if they aren't, someone will most likely be happy to pop out and bring you a beer from another place). Local beers and rum are inexpensive, but wine is a lot pricier and by-the-glass servings are often quite rough box wines.

TO HELP YOU ORDER

I would like to order…**Je voudrais commander…**

Is service included?
Est-ce que le service est compris?

I am a vegetarian **Je suis végétarien(ne)**

Do you have local specialities? **Avez-vous des spécialités locales?**

The bill please **L'addition s'il vous plait**

MENU READER

beer **bière**
bread **pain**
breakfast **le petit-déjeuner**
butter **beurre**
chicken **poulet**
coffee **café**
crab **crabe**
dinner **le dîner**
drinks **les boissons**
egg **oeuf**
fillet **filet**
fish **poisson**
fresh lemon juice served with sugar **citron pressé**
fresh squeezed orange juice **orange pressé**
garlic **ail**
herb infusion **tisane**
hot chocolate **chocolat chaud**
ice cream **crème glacée**
lamb **agneau**

lunch **le déjeuner**
meat **viande**
milk **lait**
mineral water **eau minérale**
pepper **poivre**
pork **porc**
rabbit **lapin**
red **rouge**
rice **riz**
rosé **rosé**
salt **sel**
shellfish **fruits de mer**
shrimp or prawn **crevette**
spicy **piquant**
squid **calamar**
stew **ragout**
sugar **sucre**
tea **thé**
vegetables **légumes**
vin **wine**
white **blanc**

PLACES TO EAT

We have used the following symbols to give an idea of the price of a main course for one person at budget, moderate and expensive restaurants:

€ under 5 euros
€€ 5–8 euros
€€€ over 8 euros

ANTANANARIVO AND SURROUNDS

Restaurant des Artistes € *Rue Refotana, off Avenue de l'Indépendance, tel: 034-6487931,* www.hoteldesartistes-tana.com. Popular with expats, this unpretentious brasserie boasts a shady terrace, a well-stocked bar and long menu of grills and French-style stews.

Café de la Gare €€ *Gare Soarana, Avenue de l'Indépendance, tel: 020-2261112,* www.facebook.com/cafedelagaretana. Converted from the old railway station diner, this chic central eatery has a long and varied menu. There's glassed-in terrace and garden seating, good coffee and a cosmopolitan wine list.

Kudeta Lounge-Bar Isoraka €€€ *Rue de la Réunion, tel: 020-2261140,* www.kudeta.mg. Something of a Tana institution, this stylish central trattoria has a funky decor, and a French/Italian/Malagasy fusion menu.

Restaurant Lokanga €€€ *Rue Ramboatiana, tel: 034-1455502,* www. lokanga-hotel.mg. This is the top sundowner spot in town, offering fine views over Lac Anasy. The French/Malagasy fusion menu includes the likes of zebu skewers with peanut sauce, vanilla seafood fricassée and duck in baobab sauce. Closed Mondays. Booking recommended.

Il Giardino di Lorenzo €€ *Rue Ramboatiana, tel: 020-2242776,* www.face book.com/Lorenzo.andohalo. With its homely interior and shady, this is an appealing family-run restaurant that serves excellent pizzas and pasta as well as a selection of Malagasy specials. Vegetarians are well catered for. Closed Mondays.

Grill du Rova €€ *Rue Ramboatiana, tel: 020-2262724.* www.malagasy-tours.com/grill-du-rova. Situated a few paces downhill from the Rova, this lovely terrace restaurant is the ideal place to stop for lunch between sightseeing in atmospheric Haute-Ville. The menu has a strong selection of well-priced meat- and fish-based French-Malagasy mains. Lunch only.

Restaurant La Verrière €€ *Rue Rakotonirina, tel: 020-2225945,* www.pavillondelemyrne.com. This attractive garden restaurant in the Pavillon de l'Emyrne has a shady lounge-like ambience. The well-priced menu is strong on salads, pizzas and sandwiches, supplemented by a long list of French-style meat and fish plats du jour.

Sakamanga €€ *Rue Adrianary Ratianarivo, tel: 032-0266834,* http://sakamanga.com. Decorated with black-and-white vintage photos of colonial-era Madagascar, this first-floor appendage to the eponymous hotel has a lively atmosphere, an international wine list, and a varied menu of French, Italian and Malagasy dishes. Booking recommended in the evenings.

Restaurant La Varangue €€€ *Rue Printsy Ratsimamanga, tel: 020-2227397,* www.hotel-restaurant-lavarangue-tananarive.com. Decorated with a heroically eclectic clutter of vintage bric-a-brac, this old-fashioned and rather formal hotel restaurant is renowned for its three-course set menus.

Tana Waterfront Food Court € *Tana Waterfront,* www.centre-commercial-tanawaterfront.com/food-court. From sushi to curry, pastries to burgers, Italian to Chinese, the cluster of small eateries in this pericentral mall offers great variety and good value in a spotlessly-clean environment. Closed Sunday evenings. No alcohol served.

Au Bois Vert €€ *Ambodirano, 5 minutes' drive from Ivato Airport, tel: 020-2244725,* http://auboisvert.com/en/restaurant. Set in a suburban pine plantation, this place has a cosy interior and shaded terrace seating. The specialities are pizzas, meat and seafood grilled in a wood-fired oven.

La Terrasse Auberge € *Ampefy, tel: 032-0716780,* http://laterrasse. ampefy.com. Alongside the main road through Ampefy, this friendly and down-to-earth terrace restaurant, with traditional-style decor dominated by wood and zebu skins, is the nicest place to eat in the vicinity of Lac Ifaty. Stand-out dishes are the grilled whole tilapia and chicken grilled in ginger.

Hotel-Restaurant Palissandre €€ *Rue Andriandahifotsy, tel: 020-2260560,* www.hotel-restaurant-palissandre.com. Set a stylish hotel, this terrace restaurant serves excellent French-Malagasy fare and offers a great view over the Marché Pavilions d'Analakely.

Hôtel de France € *Avenue de l'Indépendance, tel: 020-2221304.* Built in 1959, this historic hotel on bustling Avenue de l'Indépendance has seen better days, but the wide terrace bar/restaurant is a perfect place to watch can watch the city go by over a chilled beer or coffee.

ANTSIRABE

Le Pousse Café €€ *Grand Avenue, Antsirabe, tel: 034-6548761,* www. sofitrans-sa.com. Set in the historic Hôtel des Thermes, this characterful terrace restaurant overlooks the swimming pool and huge suburban garden and serves a range of French-style dishes with a Malagasy touch.

Zandina € *Avenue Foch, Antsirabe, tel: 032-6763331.* This relaxed and brightly-decorated eatery – part bistro, part sports bar –specialises in pizzas, but the long menu also includes a good selection of grills and Malagasy-style stews. There's free Wi-Fi and big screens to watch sporting events. Great value.

RANOMAFANA NATIONAL PARK

Varibolo Resto € *Varibolo ticket office, Ranomafana, tel: 034-9082303,* www.varibolo.com. Overlooking a river next to the park entrance, this friendly family-run restaurant serves tasty and filling Malagasy stews and grills to hikers.

FIANARANTSOA

Snack Imanoela € *Rue du Rova, Fianarantsoa, tel: 034-6172613,* www.facebook.com/SnackImanoela. This delightful family-run café stands in a well-maintained 19th-century homestead with a cosy interior and umbrella-shaded seating on the garden terrace. Wholesome soups and plats du jour are made with locally sourced products, and it also serves good sandwiches, homemade biscuits and coffee.

Lac Hotel €€€€ *Sahambavy, east of Fianarantsoa, tel: 020-7595906,* www.lachotel.com. Set close to Sahambavy Railway Station overlooking Lac Sahambavy and its pine-swathed shores, this large restaurant serves hearty French-style cuisine.

ISALO NATIONAL PARK

Restaurant Le Zébu Grillé €€ *RN7, Ranohira, tel: 032-4467689.* Situated at the junction for Isalo National Park, this smart little restaurant has the choice of eating in the air-conditioned interior or on a shaded terrace. The speciality, as the name suggests, is zebu steaks and brochettes, but it also serves a good selection of Malagasy stews and has the best breakfast in town.

TOLIARA AND SURROUNDS

Bo Beach Restaurant € *Boulevard Lyautey, Toliara, tel: 032-927476.* Also known as Blu, this Toliara institution has a fabulous beachfront terrace with sand underfoot. Well known for its pizzas, it also has a tempting selection of seafood and steaks, and a good cocktail menu. The bar stays open until midnight. Good value.

Auberge de la Table €€ *RN7 12km (7.5 miles) east of Toliara, tel: 032-026U015,* www.antsokayarboretum.org. Within the Arboretum d'Antsokay, this quality French-Malagasy restaurant offers the choice of sitting on a shady terrace shaded or in the cool interior. A well-priced three-course menu du jour is supplemented by à la carte meat and sea-food mains.

Chez Freddy € *Ifaty-Mangily, tel: 034-1984276.* This rustic and afford-able local eatery serves the best seafood in Ifaty-Mangily. Closed Mon-days.

FORT DAUPHIN

Talinjoo €€ *Libanona Peninsula, tel: 034-0521235,* www.talinjoo.com. No-table for its stylish contemporary decor and superb view over the bay, this exceptional restaurant offers a varied menu dominated by seafood, but also strong on burgers and pizzas. Good value.

Chez Marceline €€ *Plage d'Ankoba, tel: 032-4028715.* Boasting a won-derful beachfront location and open-air ambience, this popular eatery serves delicious seafood, zebu and chicken kebabs, all fresh from the grill and accompanied by good frites and salad.

ANDASIBE AND SURROUNDS

Hôtel Feon'ny Ala € *Tel: 020-5683202.* Ideal for a post-hike lunch on a wooden terrace overlooking a river, this popular hotel restaurant 1km (0.6 mile) from the park entrance serves a good selection of local and western dishes. Indris are often heard, but seldom seen, from the ter-race. Good value.

TOAMASINA AND SURROUNDS

Hôtel Joffre € *Boulevard Joffre, Toamasina , tel: 020-5332390,* www.hoteljoffre-tamatave.com. This characterful hotel has a beauti-fully decorated restaurant with seating that spills out onto a wide shady terrace ideal for people watching. It has an excellent and well-priced French-Malagasy menu and a long international wine list.

La Terrasse € *Boulevard Joffre,* serves a varied selection of good, cheap meals washed down with ice-cold beer or fresh coffee. The roast half-chicken with salad and frites is something of a speciality.

Azura Golf Resort €€€ *Foulpointe Golf Club,* tel: 032-0342066, www.azuragolf.mg. Situated to the north of Toamasina, this golf club and spa resort has one of the most stylish and well-regarded restaurants on the west coast. It also offers direct beach access, a modern spa, and golfing on its own 9-hole course.

MAHAJANGA

Coconut Lodge Gourmet Restaurant €€ *Avenue de France, Mahajanga,* tel: 020-6223023, www.cocolodgemajunga-madagascar.com. Run by an excellent chef, the courtyard restaurant at Hôtel Coco Lodge places a strong emphasis on organic ingredients and locally-sourced spices. Its strongest card is the superb selection of Lebanese meze and mains. The three-course set lunch is a bargain.

Chez Madame Chabaud €€ *Avenue du Général de Gaulle,* tel: 032-0706734. This homely restaurant belies its rather down-at-heel exterior with an innovative menu of French, Malagasy and Asian fusion dishes.

Alliance Française € *Boulevard Poincarré,* tel: 032-0511984, www.facebook.com/afmajunga. This hip terrace restaurant, looking out to the Corniche, is a great people-watching spot. The wallet-friendly menu includes burgers, steak and chips, samosas and chilled beer.

NOSY BE

L'Oasis € *Rue Passot, Hell-Ville,* tel: 034-7511995, www.facebook.com/oasisnosybe. Ideally placed for people-watching on Hell-Ville's most historic road, l'Oasis is an excellent retro Parisian-style café with wood-panelled walls, terracotta tile floor, wide balcony and a long menu of salads, burgers, and light meals as well as delicious coffee and cakes.

Nandipo €€ *Rue Albert I, Hell-Ville, tel: 032-2977532.* Positively exploding with character, this quirky and eclectically decorated bar-cum-bistro is housed in a two-storey Creole-style building and specialises in pizzas, pasta and seafood.

DIEGO SUAREZ AND SURROUNDS

Le Tsara de Vaovao €€€ *Rue Colbert, Diego Suarez, tel: 032-0494097.* This stylish restaurant in the heart of Diego has a down-to-earth feel and terrace seating spilling out onto the pavement. Seafood dominates the fine-dining menu. Good wine list.

Restaurant La Fleur de Sel €€ *Route de Ramena, Diego Suarez, tel: 020-8290128,* www.suarez-hotel.com. Especially strong on Mediterranean-style meat dishes and seafood, the excellent restaurant at La Suarez also serves typical Malagasy dishes. It has a pleasant open-air ambience with views into the surrounding fig trees.

L'Emeraude € *Plage de Ramena, tel: 032-5058380.* Popular with locally-based volunteers and younger travellers, this chilled beachfront restaurant, its wooden deck lapped by the waves at high tide, stands 100 metres/yds south of the jetty and serves good value fresh seafood.

A–Z TRAVEL TIPS

A SUMMARY OF PRACTICAL INFORMATION

Ⓐ Accommodation _____ 114
Admission charges _____ 114
Airports _____ 115
Ⓑ Budgeting for your
trip _____ 115
Ⓒ Car Hire _____ 116
Climate _____ 117
Clothing _____ 118
Crime and safety _____ 119
Customs regulations _____ 119
Ⓓ Disabled travellers _____ 120
Ⓔ Electricity _____ 120
Embassies and
consulates _____ 121
Emergencies _____ 122
Etiquette _____ 122
Ⓖ Guides and tours _____ 122
Ⓗ Health and medical
care _____ 123

Ⓘ Internet _____ 126
Ⓛ Language _____ 126
LGBTQ travellers _____ 127
Ⓜ Media _____ 127
Money _____ 128
Ⓞ Opening hours _____ 129
Ⓟ Postal services _____ 129
Public holidays _____ 130
Ⓡ Religious services _____ 130
Ⓣ Tax _____ 131
Telephones _____ 131
Time zone _____ 132
Toilets _____ 132
Tourist information _____ 132
Ⓥ Visas and
passports _____ 133
Ⓦ Weights and
measures _____ 133
Women travellers _____ 133

A

ACCOMMODATION

There is no shortage of accommodation in Madagascar. Truly upmarket five-star operations are thin on the ground, but there are a few isolated boutique beach and bush resorts that compare with the finest East and Southern Africa has to offer. These few luxurious anomalies aside, the trend at the upper end of the market is towards medium-small non-chain lodges, hotels and beach resorts, many of which are owner-managed, or have the informal hands-on feel of somewhere that might be. Decent accommodation of this sort can be found at pretty much all major beach resorts and large towns, as well as along the borders of the more popular national parks and protected areas. Typically, a tourist-class establishment that might nudge into the three-star category internationally would charge around €100 for a double room (usually on a bed-and-breakfast basis) while more homely and low key tourist hotels will charge around half that price, excluding breakfast. For those on a tighter budget, pensions, guesthouses and borderline-homestays aimed mainly at backpackers and/or the local market typically start at around €10.

> Do you have a single/double room for tonight? **Avez-vous une chambre pour une/deux personne(s) pour ce soir?**
> with bath/shower/toilet **avec bain/douche/toilettes**
> What's the rate per night? **Quel est le prix pour une nuit?**

ADMISSION CHARGES

Practically all formal tourist attractions charge an admission fee, almost invariably quoted and payable in the local currency (ariary). Typically, museums, cultural attractions and minor reserves charge the equivalent of €3–10 per person. National parks and other properties under Madagascar National Parks (MNP; www.parcs-madagascar.com) charge daily entrance fees equivalent to €15–20 per person, depending on the category of the individual protected area. All MNP properties and many private reserves also charge a mandatory guide fee. This varies significantly from one place to the next, and for walks of various durations, but typically it will work out at €10–30 per party per excursion. Substantial discounts are usually offered to children and to Malagasy citizens.

AIRPORTS

Antananarivo's Ivato International Airport (TNR), which stands in the eponymous suburb about 15km (9 miles) north of the city centre, is the most useful port of entry to people planning extended travels around Madagascar, as it lies in the heart of the country and is the main domestic flight hub. A good selection of international flights also services Fascene Airport (NOS) on Nosy Be and a limited choice of international flights services Sainte-Marie Airport (SMS) on the offshore resort of Île Sainte-Marie. Airport taxes are usually included in ticket fares.

Where can I get a taxi? **Où puis-je trouver un taxi?**
How much is it to Antananarivo town centre **Quel est le prix de la course jusqu'au centre d'Antananarivo?**
Does this bus go to Antananarivo? **Est-ce que cet autobus va à Antananarivo?**

B

BUDGETING FOR YOUR TRIP

Most visitors are on pre-booked trips that include transport, accommodation, guides and some or all meals and activities, in which case the only ad hoc expenses are likely to be tips, drinks, souvenirs and the occasional meal. For independent travellers, Madagascar can be very cheap or extremely expensive, depending, among other things, on whether you get around by taxi-brousse (nominal fares) or air (most legs are around €250 one-way), eat at local or tourist-oriented restaurants, and sleep in local guesthouses or bona fide tourist hotels, as well as how much you opt to spend on organised activities such as day walks in national parks, diving or snorkelling and the like.

Within Madagascar, most prices are quoted in the local currency, the ariary. However, this is prone to ongoing devaluation against harder currencies, a trend reflected in the corresponding inflation of most local goods in line with the Euro (as opposed to the US dollar or pound sterling).

Sample costs

A local beer: From under €1 per 500ml bottle in a supermarket to around €2–3 in a posh restaurant or hotel

A glass of house wine: €2–4

A main course at a budget/moderate/expensive restaurant: €2–4/€5–8/€10–15

A room in a cheap/moderate/deluxe hotel: €10–25/€30–60/€80–200

A taxi journey to and from the main airport for the destination: €10–20

C

CAR HIRE

Most car rental companies and tour companies offer chauffeured cars only, partly due to insurance regulations, partly because the poor condition of the roads and the assertive (read: reckless) local driving style are daunting to most foreigners. If you do arrange a self-drive vehicle, you will need an international driving license, and must be at least 23 years old. Be aware that filling stations are few and far between. Be alert to the risk of dopy or drunk pedestrians, or livestock (in particular zebu cattle) sauntering unexpectedly across the road.

I'd like to rent a car **J'aimerais louer une voiture...**

...tomorrow/for one day/week **demain/pour un jour/ semaine.**

Please include full insurance **Veuillez inclure une assurance complète.**

Driving licence **permis de conduire**

Car registration papers **carte grise**

Are we on the right road for...? **Sommes-nous sur la route de...?**

Fill the tank, please. **Le plein, s'il vous plaît.**

I've broken down. **Ma voiture est en panne.**

There's been an accident. **Il y a eu un accident.**

CLIMATE

Madagascar experiences wide regional variations in climate, with the temperate highlands of the interior generally being significantly cooler and less humid than the coast. Rainfall in highest in the east and lowest in the southwest, which means that seasonal considerations are more of a factor when visiting the east coast than the far southwest. The selected climate charts will give you a good idea of seasonal weather conditions by region, but for most visitors, the broad advice outlined below will apply countrywide.

Summer (December to March)

The weather is hot and humid countrywide, with high rainfall in most regions, but particularly the east coast, which is also frequently hit by cyclones at this time of year. The high rainfall makes it the least attractive time of year to travel in Madagascar, as many national parks become inaccessible, wildlife is difficult to locate in the dense foliage, and some lodges close for the season. On the plus side, the countryside tends to be very lush during the rainy season, and most hotels offer negotiable discounts.

Autumn/early winter (April to June)

The weather is hot and humid on the coast, with some rainfall, but cooler and drier upcountry. The countryside remains green after the rainy season, but most roads are passable and national parks accessible. Tourist arrival numbers are low in April but start building toward high season volumes over the course of late May into June. Overall this is an excellent time to visit Madagascar.

Midwinter (July and August)

The weather is similar to that from April to June, but drier and slightly cooler. Climatically there is no finer time to visit Madagascar, but it is also peak tourist season, since it coincides with summer school holidays in the northern hemisphere. As a result, hotels tend to charge inflated seasonal rates, and parks and other natural attractions can become unpleasantly busy with noisy tour parties and families. If peace and quiet are high on your priority list , avoid this time of year.

Late winter/spring (September to November)

The weather is similar to April to June, but tourist volumes are down from midwinter. Overall this is also a great time of year to travel in all parts of Madagascar.

	J	F	M	A	M	J	J	A	S	O	N	D
max °C	30	30	31	28	27	25	24	24	27	30	31	32
max °F	86	86	88	82	81	77	75	75	81	86	88	90
min °C	16	18	17	16	16	15	12	12	15	17	17	15
min °F	61	64	62	61	61	59	54	54	59	62	62	59

CLOTHING

Light summery clothes are the order of the day along the coast, but you'll need a sweater, jacket or sweatshirt for the evenings, as it often gets quite windy. Antananarivo and other highlands destinations can get unexpectedly chilly at night, so you will want long trousers and a few layers of warm clothing. Other essentials year-round are a good sunhat and decent rain gear for rainforest walks. Open sandals or flip-flops are fine for beach destinations, but trainers are the minimum requirement for forest and other walks, and proper walking or hiking boots are preferable. Local dress codes are very informal but it is unacceptable for women to go topless on beaches, so bring a bikini.

CRIME AND SAFETY

Violent crime against tourists remains a rarity in most parts of the country. The one major exception is Batterie Beach north of Toliara, which should be avoided at all costs following several violent attacks and fatalities. Parts of Antananarivo are also risky at night, and nocturnal road travel outside urban areas carries a risk of bandit attacks. Elsewhere, snatch theft and pickpocketing are no more than a minor risk provided you take the usual commonsense precautions i.e. never wear ostentatious jewellery, leave valuables lying around your hotel rooms, or walk alone on unlit alleys after dark. Before you travel, log onto the FCO (www.fco.gov.uk) and US state department (https://travel.state.gov) for the latest official advice and news about periodic unrest or outbreaks of disease.

On the road, the safest place for your passport, tickets and excess money is the hotel safe, or a well concealed money-belt. Malagasy law dictates that you carry your passport, or a certified copy, on your person at all times. A certified passport copy can be obtained by taking the original and a photocopy to any police station.

Where's the nearest police station? **Où est le commissariat de police le plus proche?**

CUSTOMS REGULATIONS

Visitors and residents are allowed the free import of 500 cigarettes or 25 cigars or 500 grams of tobacco, as well as 1 bottle of alcoholic beverage.

Visitors and residents can import up to 400,000 Malagasy ariary in local currency, and an unlimited amount of foreign currency, though any sum of money greater than €7,500 must be declared at customs.

Visitors and residents can export up to 400,000 Malagasy ariary in local currency and an unlimited amount of foreign cash, but a written declaration of all money exported must be made at customs.

Import of the following items is prohibited: illegal drugs, weapons, explosives and ammunition, knives and other deadly weapons, counterfeit money and goods, electronic equipment, pornographic materials, and plant, meat or other animal products.

> I've nothing to declare **Je n'ai rien à déclarer.**
> It's for my personal use **C'est pour mon usage personnel.**

D

DISABLED TRAVELLERS

Madagascar has few facilities for disabled travellers and travel conditions are generally not conducive to those with limited mobility. Most tour operators will do their best to smooth things for visitors with disabilities, but even then you may find that hotels advertising disabled rooms are guilty of overstating the case. Few multi-storeyed hotels have lifts and bungalow accommodation is often accessed via narrow rocky paths or outside staircases.

E

ELECTRICITY

Standard voltage is 220 V and standard frequency is 50Hz. The most common power socket is the standard European plug with two round pins. Some hotels have other sockets, however, so it is worth carrying an adaptor set wherever you are coming from.

> I need an adaptor/a battery, please. **J'ai besoin d'un adaptateur/ une pile s'il vous plaît**

EMBASSIES AND CONSULATES

Foreign representatives in Madagascar

Australia represented by Australian High Commission: 2nd Floor, Rogers House, 5 President John Kennedy Street, Port Louis, Mauritius, tel: +230-2020160, http://mauritius.embassy.gov.au

Canada: Ivandry Business Centre, Rue Velo Rainimangalahy, Antananarivo, tel: 020-2243256, http://www.canadainternational.gc.ca/south-africa-afriquedusud/contact-antananarivo-contactez.aspx

France: Rue Jean-Jaurès, Antananarivo, tel: 020-2239850, https://mg.ambafrance.org

Ireland: c/o Embassy of Ireland, 2nd Floor, Parkdev Building, Brooklyn Bridge Office Park, 570 Fehrsen Street, Pretoria 0181, South Africa, tel: +27 12 452 1000, www.dfa.ie/embassies/irish-embassies-abroad/sub-saharan-africa/madagascar

South Africa: Rue Ravoninahitriniarivo, Antananarivo, tel: 020-2243350, http://www.dirco.gov.za/madagascar

UK: Rue Ravoninahitriniarivo, Antananarivo 101, tel: 020-2233053, www.gov.uk/world/organisations/british-embassy-antananarivo

USA: Lot 207 Andranoro-Antehiroka, Antananarivo, tel: 020-2348000, https://mg.usembassy.gov

Malagasy embassies and consulates abroad

Australia: Level 9, 47 York Street, Sydney, NSW 2000, tel: +61 (0)2-92992290

Canada: 03 Rue Raymond, Ottawa, tel: +613-567 0505, http://madagascar-embassy.ca

France: 4 Avenue Raphaël, Paris, tel: +33 (0)1 45 04 62 11, www.ambassade-madagascar.com

South Africa: 77 Newlands Ave, Cape Town, tel: + 27 (0)21-6747238 www.madagascarconsulate.org.za

UK: c/o 4 Avenue Raphaël, Paris, tel: +33 (0)1 45 04 62 11, www.ambassade-madagascar.com
USA: 2374 Massachusetts Ave, Washington DC, tel: +1 202-265 5525, www.madagascar-embassy.org

EMERGENCIES
Police: 17 or 117 from a mobile phone.
Fire Brigade: 18 or 118 from a mobile phone.
Gendarmerie: 19 or 119 from a mobile phone.
Ambulance and medical: 17 (117 from mobile phone) or 020-2235753

ETIQUETTE
The most important point of etiquette is to respect local *fady* (taboos), the most significant and universal of which not to point at things, but to indicate the required direction with your knuckle and index finger crooked backwards. Although Madagascar is predominantly Christian and traditional, it is conventional (as in Muslim and Hindu countries) to reserve the left hand for ablutions and the right hand for eating and passing things. Greetings are not significantly different to most Western countries: men and sometimes women usually shake hands upon greeting. If you are invited to visit Malagasy people at home, it is customary to bring a bottle of rum as a gift.

G

GUIDES AND TOURS
Tour operators
Most visitors make all their arrangements through a local or specialist international tour operator such as Insight Guides, which offers ready-made and customisable trips to all the best locations in Madagascar devised by our local experts. Browse our exciting selection on www.insightguides.com/tour/Madagascar.

Well-established local companies that contributed significantly to the research of this guidebook and can be unreservedly recommended are as follows:

Malagasy Tours Tel: 020-2235607, www.malagasy-tours.com
Mora Travel Tel. 020-2202012 or 085-8772236, www.moratravel.com
Za Tours Tel: 020-2242286, www.zatours-madagascar.com

H

HEALTH AND MEDICAL CARE

It is vital that your travel insurance policy is comprehensive and includes emergency evacuation and repatriation, as medical care in Madagascar does not conform to European and North American standards. If you are on medication, make sure you carry enough to last you, plus a prescription and letter from your doctor.

Health advice In the UK, detailed health advice, tailored to individual needs, is available from Medical Advice for Travellers Abroad (MASTA; www.masta-travel-health.com. Traveller advice is also available on the NHS website (www.fitfortravel.nhs.uk) and the International Association for the Medical Assistance of Travellers (IAMAT; www.iamat.org), which also provides members (membership is free) with health information and a list of approved doctors all over the world.

Inoculations Consult your doctor about inoculations at least two months before you leave. Yellow fever is not present in Madagascar but an inoculation may be required if you are travel from or via an infected area. Diphtheria, polio and tetanus vaccinations are also a good idea. Meningitis, typhoid and hepatitis A and B inoculations are recommended, especially for longer stays.

Rabies vaccinations are usually only given if you are likely to be in close contact with animals during your stay.

First-aid kit
The following items should be in your first-aid kit: strong mosquito

repellent; malaria prophylactics; sting-relief cream; antihistamine pills; plasters, antiseptic wipes and spray for blisters and cuts; syringes; Imodium for diarrhoea. Also, take your own condoms and tampons (if required).

Hygiene

Many areas in Madagascar are subject to occasional outbreaks of cholera and dysentery due to poor sanitation and hygiene. Be conscientious about washing your hands regularly with soap and water and ensure that you drink from a safe supply. Wash all fresh food thoroughly in boiled or bottled water before you eat it.

Sun protection

The tropical sun is strong, so sunblock and a head covering – ideally a wide-brimmed hat – are mandatory for those coming from temperate climates.

Health risks

HIV/AIDS infection rates are low by comparison to mainland Africa, but other STDs are rife, so avoid high-risk activities such as unprotected sex.

Bilharzia This nasty disease is transmitted by flukes that live in snails that like still, well-vegetated freshwater habitats. Sea water is safe, as are swimming pools and fast-flowing streams or rivers, but all other inland freshwater bodies should be viewed as suspect.

Diarrhoea Be fastidious about drinking and brushing your teeth with purified or bottled water. Diarrhoea usually clears itself up within a few days. If there is no sign of improvement within 48 hours, it could be caused by a parasite or infection, so get to a doctor.

Malaria The most serious health risk to travellers, malaria is transmitted by the female anopheles mosquito, a nocturnal and crepuscular species that is usually most active at dusk and dawn. The risk of contraction is highest in the rainy season, when mosquitos are most active, and along the coast and other low-lying areas, but it could happen almost anywhere in Madagascar at any time. Seek advice about the most suitable medication for you and your family from your doctor or a tropical medicine institute at least two months before your departure. No drug offers 100 percent protection, so cover up in the evening, make liberal use of insect repellent, and sleep in screened room under a mosquito net. If you start displaying possible malarial symptoms within six months of your return home, consult a doctor, and be sure to tell them where you have been travelling.

Automobile accidents Car crashes are a leading cause of injury among travellers to Madagascar, so walk and drive defensively, wear a seat belt and avoid travelling at night.

Snakebite Madagascar has no snake or spiders that pose a significant health threat – its few venomous snakes are all back-fanged biters, and could do damage only if you literally inserted a finger in their mouth.

Health care and hospitals

There are some good private clinics, hospitals and other medical practitioners in Antananarivo. Elsewhere, facilities are more basic and unreliable. In a real emergency, you might consider being flown to South Africa, which has world-class private medical facilities. The following are recommended:

Polyclinique Ilafy RN3, 5km (3 miles) north of the city centre, tel: 020-2242566 or 033-1107391, www.sodiatgroupe.mg/polyclinique-ilafy.php. This large 24-hour clinic is equipped with several ambulances and can handle most medical emergencies.

Espace Médical Ambodivona Tana Waterfront, RN3, tel: 020 2262566 or 034-0200911, email: esmed@moov.mg. Another good 24-hour clinic and hospital equipped to deal with medical emergencies.

Pharmacie Métropole 7 Rue Ratsimilaho Antaninarenina, tel: 020-2267522 or 033-1520025, www.pharmacie-metropole.com. Well-stocked and central pharmacy open Mon–Sat 8.30am–12.30pm and 2–6.30pm

Pharmacie d'Isoraka Avenue du Général Ramanantsoa, tel: 020-2269412, www.facebook.com/pharmacieisoraka. Set in the old central suburb of Isoraka, this is open daily 8am–noon and 2–6pm.

INTERNET

Most hotels and many smarter restaurants and cafés in Antananarivo and other large towns and beach resorts offer free Wi-Fi to clients. Wi-Fi is less widely available in more remote areas such as lodges bordering national parks. Even where it is readily available, Internet tends to be quite slow, and dips in service are commonplace. If you are likely to need regular Internet connectivity, buy a local SIM card and data bundle (both very inexpensive) with one of the mobile phone providers listed under the Telephone section.

L

LANGUAGE

The official languages of Madagascar are French and Malagasy. English is also quite widely spoken by guides, hotel receptionists, restaurant staff and other working within the tourist industry, but not by the average Malagasy. French is sufficient to get around in towns and other places that regularly receive tourists, but in more rural areas it may be useful – and will win you plenty of friends – to know a few words of Malagasy.

0 **aotra**	6 **enina**
1 **iraika**	7 **fito**
2 **roa**	8 **valo**
3 **telo**	9 **sivy**
4 **efatra**	10 **folo**
5 **dimy**	100 **zato**

Hello **Manao ohoana (or Salama)**
Goodbye **Veloma**
Please/Excuse me **Asafady**
Thank you **Misaotra**

Help **Vonjeo**
Do you speak English/French? **Miteny Anglisy/Frantsay ve ianao?**
Yes **Eny**
No **Tsia**
What is your name? **Iza no anaranao**
My name is... **Ny anarako dia...**
Do you have...? **Misy...ve?**
How much does it cost? **Ohatrinona ny vidin'ity?**
Where is...? **Aiza no misy?**
Market **tsena**
Shop **fivarotana**

LGBTQ TRAVELLERS

Madagascar is unusual in Africa insofar as same-sex sexual activity is legal, provided both parties are at least 21 years of age. However, societal discrimination against the LGBTQ community remains strong, and there are no laws prohibiting hate speech or discrimination of this sort. Same-sex marriage is not recognised. Gay and lesbian travellers are unlikely to face any problems provided they avoid public displays of affection.

M

MEDIA

There is no English-language press in Madagascar. Of the four main daily newspapers, the Madagascar Tribune (www.madagascar-tribune.com) is of greatest interest as the only one with exclusively French content, the others are all a mix of French and Malagasy. For international news, check international news websites such as www.bbc.com online.

The main radio broadcaster is the state-owned Radio Nationale Malagasy (RNM), which has a countrywide and dominates the airwaves in rural areas. A few private broadcasters operate in Antananarivo and other large towns. Coverage is entirely in Malagasy and French.

The main terrestrial television broadcaster Television Malagasy (TVM) tends towards the parochial and only operates in Malagasy and French. Most hotels also offer a bouquet of satellite channels either with the French-dominated Canal+ or predominantly Anglophone South African service DSTV.

MONEY

The local currency is the Malagasy ariary (MGA), which was also the local name for a silver dollar in pre-colonial times. It was introduced in 1961 at the equivalent of five Malagasy francs, and banknotes were denominated in both currencies until the franc was officially discontinued in 2005. Bank notes are issued in denominations of MGA 100, 200, 500, 1,000, 5,000 and 10,000, which at the current exchange rate means that the largest note is equivalent to roughly €3, US$3 or £2.50!

The easiest way to access money is to draw local currency from ATMs using a credit or debit card. Visa and Mastercard can be used at ATMs attached to most major banks. The most reliable option appears to be the Banque Fampandrosoana ny Varotra-Société Générale (BFV-SG; look out for the prominent red signpost). Most ATMs limit withdrawals to MGA 300,000 or 400,000, but you can make several successive withdrawals. ATM facilities are usually available only in larger towns, so carry some hard currency cash as a backup - the euro is the most widely-recognised currency, but the US dollar, British pound and South African rand are also widely accepted.

Tipping is a way of life in Madagascar. Most drivers, guides, porters and other locals who provide a service will expect a tip as a matter of course. A small note (up to MGA 500) should suffice in the case of a porter, but guides would expect a sum equivalent to

5–15 percent of the official park or guide fee, while up to €5 per day would be good for a driver. Tipping is not customary in small local eateries or bars, but you might want to leave any small change for the waiter or waitress. In more formal restaurants, a 5–10 percent tip is customary.

> Could you give me some (small) change? **Pouvez-vous me donner de la (petite) monnaie?**
> I want to change some pounds/dollars. **Je voudrais changer des livres sterling/des dollars.**
> Can I pay with this credit card? **Puis-je payer avec cette carte de crédit?**

O

OPENING HOURS

Shops, museums and other such institutions typically open Monday to Friday from 8am or 9am to 5pm or 6pm, but many close for lunch for at least an hour between noon and 2pm. Many small shops stay open over the weekend but others close on Sunday. Banking hours are 8am–4pm. Banks and offices almost invariably close over weekends and on public holidays.

P

POSTAL SERVICES

The national postal service Paositra Malagasy (www.paositramalagasy. mg) has post offices in most large towns. International mail is slow and unreliable, so any items of important or value are best entrusted to a courier such as DHL (tel: 020-2242839 or 034-4217777; www.dhl.com/ en/mg/country_profile.html).

Express (special delivery) **par exprès**
Airmail **par avion**
Registered **en recommandé**
Have you any mail for...? **Avez-vous du courrier pour...?**

PUBLIC HOLIDAYS

Banks and government offices generally close on public holidays, as do some retail businesses. Where a public holiday falls over a weekend, the following Monday may be treated as a holiday. Fixed date public holidays are listed below. Variable-date holidays recognised countrywide are Easter Sunday and Monday, Ascension Thursday and Whit Sunday and Monday. The Islamic holidays Id al Fitr and Id al Adha are taken by Muslims only.

1 January New Year's Day
8 March Women's Day
29 March Martyrs' Day
1 May Labour Day
26 June Independence Day
15 August Assumption Day
1 November All Saints' Day
25 December Christmas Day

R

RELIGIOUS SERVICES

Catholicism, Protestantism and Islam are all widely practiced, as are traditional religions. Most towns have at least one Catholic, Anglican and/or Lutheran church that holds a service on Sunday mornings. The concept of atheism is rather unfamiliar to the Malagasy, but many are pantheists who combine traditional and Christian beliefs.

T

TAX

A Value-Added Tax (VAT) of 20 percent is levied on many items and services, but it is invariably incorporated into the asking price and thus hidden from the consumer. The same goes for duties on items such as alcoholic beverages and cigarettes.

TELEPHONES

The international dialling code for Madagascar is +261. All local numbers contain 10 numerals. There are no area codes as such, but land lines start with '020' while mobile numbers start with '03'. In both case the leading zero is dropped when dialling from outside the country (so a local number 020-xxxxxxx is dialled as +261-20-xxxxxxx from abroad).

Madagascar has a good mobile network and it is well worth making the minor investment required to buy a local SIM card, airtime and a data bundle for internet browsing, downloading emails and using apps such as whatsapp, facebook and facetime. Orange Madagascar (www.orange.mg) offers the best service within Antananarivo but the state-owned Telma (www.telma.mg) has a more extensive countrywide network into remote areas. Both have kiosks at the airport where you can set yourself up within a few minutes of landing.

International dialling codes out of Madagascar

Australia: +61
Canada: +1
Ireland: +353
New Zealand: +64
South Africa: +27
UK: +44
USA: +1

TIME ZONE

Madagascar is in the Eastern Africa time zone (GMT/UST+3), which means it is three hours ahead of the UK in winter and two hours ahead in summer, and 7–9 hours ahead of the mainland USA. Because it lies so close to the tropics, the difference in the duration of summer and winter daylight is relatively minimal. But it is a lot further east than most of East Africa, which means the sun tends to rise/set rather early (daylight hours range from around 5am–5.45pm in December to 6.30am–5.20pm in June).

TOILETS

Western-style flush toilets are the norm, but some bush camps might have squat or long-drop toilets. Public toilets are not readily available.

Where is the toilet? **Où sont les toilettes?**

TOURIST INFORMATION

The Office National du Tourisme de Madagascar (ONTM; tel: 020-2266115) operates an informative website https://madagascar-tourisme.com/en. Also useful is the website maintained by Madagascar National Parks (MNP; tel: 034-4941538; www.parcs-madagascar.com), which details more than 40 protected areas countrywide. Many regional tourist offices operate good websites. These include the following:

Antananarivo: www.tourisme-antananarivo.com
Antsirabe: www.antsirabe-tourisme.com
Fianarantsoa: www.tourisme-fianara.com
Morondava: www.morondavatourisme.com
Fort Dauphin: www.fort-dauphin.org
Île Sainte-Marie: http://saintemarie-tourisme.mg
Mahajanga: www.majunga.org
Nosy Be: www.nosybe-tourisme.com
Diego Suarez: www.office-tourisme-diego-suarez.com

V

VISAS AND PASSPORTS

All visitors must be in possession of a passport valid for at least six months after their intended departure date and with at least one page empty. Visas are required by all visitors. Single-entry tourist visas valid for up to 90 days can be bought without fuss at the two main international airports and cost the MGA equivalent of around €20/30/40 for 30/60/90 days. Multiple-entry and business or other non-tourist visas must be arranged in advance through a Madagascar embassy or consulate.

W

WEIGHTS AND MEASURES

Madagascar uses metric measurements.

WOMEN TRAVELLERS

Single female travellers generally have a positive experience in Madagascar and they face few risks specific to their gender. That said, as would be the case almost anywhere in the world, they can expect to attract the interest of single men, but perhaps slightly more so due to the image of promiscuity associated with films and other western media. It will help deflect attention to dress modestly, to wear a wedding ring, and to tell anybody who cares to ask that you are married and have a husband waiting somewhere. On public transport, try so sit next to another woman. It is unusual for mild flirtation or curiosity to escalate into something more threatening or persistent but in the unlikely event it does, try to enlist the support of a local woman or older man.

RECOMMENDED HOTELS

Most tourists visit Madagascar on organised tours, where all accommodation is booked by the tour operator. For independent travellers, you can either make an email reservation directly with the hotel or through online sites such as www.airbnb.com and www.booking.com. Hotels at the upper end of the market, charging upwards of 100 euros a night, are predominantly located in well-known beach resorts, the national parks and larger towns. At the other end of the spectrum, no-frills guesthouses, charming family-run lodges and budget hotels are found across the country and many represent extremely good value, at less than 25 euros a night.

The following price codes are based on the rate of a standard double room, which is usually exclusive of breakfast in Madagascar.

€€€€	over 100 euros
€€€	50-100 euros
€€	25-50 euros
€	under 25 euros

ANTANANARIVO AND SURROUNDS

Lokanga Boutique Hotel €€€€ *Rue Ramboatiana, tel: 034-1455502,* www.lokanga-hotel.mg. Situated in a historic two-storey house built in 1930 to house the royal musicians, this classy hotel consist of just five rooms with a feel that evokes Paris between the wars. Around the corner from the old Rova, it offers superb views across Lac Anasy.

Guesthouse Maison Vue Royale €€€ *Rue Printsy Kamamy, tel: 034-2038838,* www.vueroyale.com. This small family-run hotel stands in historic Haut-Ville and, as its name suggests, offers fine views over the city centre and surrounding hills. Modern rooms with air-conditioning, TV and private balconies.

Hotel Colbert €€€€ *Rue Printsy Ratsimamanga, tel: 020-2220202,* www. hotel-restaurant-colbert.com. This historic 150-room hotel has a grand reception hall with classical art on the walls and an air of studied hauteur. Carpeted rooms are slightly old-fashioned but come with all mod cons. Amenities include an indoor pool and wellness centre.

Sakamanga From €/€€ without/with AC *Rue Adrianary Ratianarivo, tel: 032-0266834,* http://sakamanga.com. This likeable budget hotel feels like a mini-museum with all manner of old Malagasy artefacts and artworks. Other attributes include hands-on owner-managers, a swimming pool area with bar, two excellent restaurants, and well-maintained rooms that cater to all budgets.

Gassy Country House €€ *Off Mamory Ivato Road, tel: 034-1425496,* www. gassycountryhouse.mg. Also known as Island Continent (IC), this attractively-priced small hotel has bright, spacious rooms and a lovely swimming pool area. Close to the airport and offering free transfers, it is perfect for overnight stays between flights.

ANTSIRABE

Couleur Café €€ *Rue d'Ambositra, Antsirabe, tel: 020-4448526,* www. couleurcafeantsirabe.com. Set in leafy gardens on the outskirts of Antsirabe, this boutique lodge offers accommodation in comfortable bungalows with TV and log fire.

AMBOSITRA

Hôtel Mania € *Rue du Commerce, Ambositra, tel: 034-9747890.* This friendly, central hotel is split across two buildings separated by a garden courtyard. The old wing oozes character with ornate Zafimaniry-carved balconies. The new wing is rather more mundane.

RANOMAFANA NATIONAL PARK

Karibotel €€ *RN25, Ranomafana National Park, tel: 033-1562951,* www. karibotel.mg. Set in sloping gardens opposite the Ranomafana River, this well-priced lodge has 13 colourful chalets with wide balconies. Ask for a front-row chalet for the best view.

Club La Vanille *8km south of Manakara, tel: 020-7221023,* www.facebook. com/Lavanillemanakara. This seaside sibling of the central Hotel La Vanille has a wonderfully isolated location on a lovely swimming beach. Accommodation is in spacious two-storey thatched houses with private balcony. Great seafood, too. €€

FIANARANTSOA

Lac Hotel €€€€ *Sahambavy, east of Fianarantsoa, tel: 020-7595906,* www.lachotel.com. This charming lakeside hotel has a large restaurant warmed by a log-fire and rooms that include some wonderful stilted wooden units whose balconies dangle above the lake. One of the best and prettiest hotels in the central highlands.

ISALO NATIONAL PARK

ITC Lodge € *Ranohira, 500 metres/yds along the road to Isalo National Park, tel: 032-4570336,* www.itclodge-isalo.com. This attractive lodge offers accommodation in rustic wooden chalets and a great restaurant. Good base for exploring Isalo.

MORONDAVA

Chez Maggie €€€ *Morondava Beach, tel: 020-9552347,* www.chez maggie.com. Morondava's best-known hotel boasts a delightful beachfront location, comfortable accommodation in modern, individually-styled thatched chalets and a top-notch restaurant.

TOLIARA AND SURROUNDS

Manatane Hotel € *Boulevard Lyautey, Toliara, tel: 034-0230909,* www. hoteltulear-manatane.com. This characterful and well-run seafront budget hotel has well-priced first-floor rooms with private sea-facing balcony, twin bed, fitted net and fan.

Arboretum d'Antsokay €€ *RN7 12km (7.5 miles) east of Toliara, tel: 032-0260015*, www.antsokayarboretum.org. Highly recommended to nature lovers, the spacious air-conditioned bungalows at this excellent arboretum are attractively located in a spiny desert setting. A swimming pool is attached.

Hôtel Le Paradisier €€€€ *Ifaty, 3km (2 miles) south of Mangily, tel: 032-0766009*, www.paradisier.net. This superb eco-lodge has an isolated location in expansive grounds that combine a seafront location with a spiny forest interior, run through by several walking trails. The well-equipped two-storey units are the ultimate in barefoot chic, and the smart open-sided restaurant serves fine seafood with a sea-view.

FORT DAUPHIN AND SURROUNDS

Hôtel Lavasoa €€ *Libanona Peninsula, Fort Dauphin, tel: 033-1251703*, www.lavasoa.com. Boasting a delightful clifftop location above the popular Libanona Beach, this unpretentious lodge offers accommodation in six wooden cabins with a private or shared balcony offering fine views across the bay.

Talinjoo Hotel €€€ *Libanona Peninsula, Fort Dauphin, tel: 034-0521235*, www.talinjoo.com. This funky modern hotel has 14 large comfortable rooms, an infinity pool overlooking the spectacular Fausse-Baie des Galions and an exceptional restaurant.

Manafiafy Lodge €€€€ *Baie de Sainte-Luce, tel: 020-2202226*, www.madaclassic.com. A contender for Madagascar's most idyllic and exclusive beach lodge, Manafiafy stands in glorious isolation on a beautiful bay. The massive wood-and-palm-frond chalets are carved into the bush for privacy, and all have a private deck with shower and sun-loungers. Activities include forest walks, snorkelling, kayaking, motorboat trips into the mangroves and whale-watching from June to December. Rates are inclusive of superb seafood meals, wine and beer, and activities.

Berenty Lodge €€€€ *Réserve de Bérenty, tel: 032-0541698*, www.madagascar-resorts.com. This popular lodge has functional bungalows with modern amenities, but it is mainly of interest for the opportunity to get up close to the lemurs and other wildlife of Réserve de Bérenty.

Mandrare River Camp €€€€ *Mandrare Valley, tel: 020-2202226,* www.madaclassic.com. Tucked away on the west bank of the eponymous river, this replica of a classic African tented camp offers a full-on 'safari' experience, including expertly-guided walking excursions within the Ifotaka Community Forest Reserve. Rates are inclusive of superb meals, wine and beer, and all activities.

ANDASIBE AND SURROUNDS

Hotel Feon'ny Ala €€ *Tel: 020-5683202.* This busy 40-bungalow lodge has a wonderful location overlooking a river and forest alive with birds. The comfortable thatched bungalows have private balconies, some with river view. Exceptional value.

Vakona Forest Lodge €€€ *Tel: 020-2262480,* www.hotelvakona.com. Vakona is the most upmarket option in the vicinity, with an attractive restaurant overlooking a small artificial lake and amenities including a spa, horseback trips and access to Lemur Island.

PANGALANES

Hôtel Palmarium €€€ *Lac Ampitabe, tel: 034-1772977,* www.palmarium.biz. A wildlife lover's paradise, this isolated lakeshore retreat is overrun with diurnal lemurs and is also a great birdwatching site and base for night trips to Île au Coq. Accommodation is in spacious rustic wooden chalets with wide balconies.

TOAMASINA

Hôtel Joffre €€ *Boulevard Joffre, tel: 020-5332390,* www.hoteljoffre-tamatave.com. The most characterful and central place to stay in Toamasina is this restored colonial hotel whose 35 spacious rooms are attractively decorated with a combination of modern art and vintage posters.

MAHAMBO

La Pirogue €€ *Mahambo Beach, tel: 033-0876810,* www.lapirogue-hotel.com. The focus of tourist activity in Mahambo, La Pirogue has comfortable thatched bungalows scattered around large beachfront gardens. There's a breezy beachfront seafood restaurant and activities include table tennis, billiards, darts, kayaking, quad-bike rental and seasonal whale-watching trips. Excellent value.

ÎLE SAINTE-MARIE

Sambatra Beach Lodge €€€ *Île aux Nattes, tel: 033-7683499,* www.sambatrabeachlodge.com. Set in lovely palm-shaded beachfront grounds, this lodge offers a barefoot luxury experience in thatched stone bungalows with private balcony and direct beach access.

Princess Bora Lodge & Spa €€€€ *Île Sainte-Marie, tel: 032-0709048,* www.princesse-bora.com. This wonderfully luxurious lodge comprises 20 large and airy thatched beach villas with crisp modern decor, king-size beds with fitted nets, private balconies with hammock, and lushly-vegetated surrounds to ensure privacy.

Masoala Forest Lodge €€€€ *Parc National de Masoala, tel: 032-0541587,* www.masoalaforestlodge.com. Accessible only by foot or sea, this stylish, award-winning eco-lodge stands in a private concession within Masoala National Park. The naturally ventilated wood-and-thatch treehouses and beach-chalets take a maximum of 14 guests.

PARC NATIONAL D'ANKARAFANTSIKA

Blue Vanga Lodge €€ *400 metres/yds from the RN4 at Andranofasika, tel: 034-0852222,* www.bluevanga-lodge.com. The most attractive base for walks in Ankarafantsika, this comfortable private lodge consists of half-a-dozen en suite thatched bungalows with nets and small shady private balconies.

MAHAJANGA

Hôtel Coco Lodge €€€ *Avenue de France, tel: 020-6223023*, www.coco lodgemajunga-madagascar.com. Centrally located just 200 metres/yds from the Corniche, this modern hotel is built around a leafy swimming pool and outstanding courtyard restaurant. Unusually spacious rooms have AC, satellite TV and fridge.

NOSY BE

Nosy Lodge €€€€ *Ambondrona Beach, tel: 032-4045204*, www.nosy-lodge.com. This well-run, family-owned lodge has large rooms, each with a private balcony and sea view, as well as a lovely beachside swimming pool.

Constance Tsarabanjina €€€€ *Nosy Tsarabanjina, tel: 034-0215229*, www.constancehotels.com. This fly-in no-frills 25-villa lodge occupies a gorgeous and otherwise uninhabited island in the Mitsio Archipelago northeast of Nosy Be.

Tsara Komba €€€€ *Nosy Komba, tel: 032-0744040*, www.tsarakomba.com. Perched on a forested slope running down to the southern shore of Nosy Komba, this back-to-nature four-star lodge offers accommodation in large, individually-styled wood and palm thatch bungalows with wide balconies facing a beautiful isolated swimming beach. Wildlife is plentiful.

DIÉGO SUAREZ

La Suarez €€€ *Route de Ramena, Diego Suarez, tel: 020-8290128*, www.suarez-hotel.com. Situated on a well-wooded slope above Baie des Français on the eastern outskirts of Diego, this charming and tranquil beach hotel has classy but unpretentious Mediterranean-style architecture, a great swimming pool and a fine spa and restaurant.

Hôtel Lakana €€ *Plage de Ramena, tel: 032-5621447*, www.lakana-hotel-ramena.com. Set in an isolated patch of bush 100 metres/yds from the beach and five minutes' walk from central Ramena, this comfortable lodge offers accommodation in cool palm-thatch bungalows with nets, AC or fan, and shaded balconies. A swimming pool and good open-air restaurant are attached. It's a family friendly set-up and popular with kitesurfers.

MONTAGNE D'AMBRE

Nature Lodge €€€€ *Joffreville, tel: 034-2012306,* www.naturelodge-ambre.com. A popular base for exploring nearby Parc National de la Montagne d'Ambre, Nature Lodge consists of 12 airy wooden bungalows spaced out in large gardens to offer privacy and a fine view from the balconies over nearby hills. Excellent three-course meals.

RÉSERVE SPÉCIALE D'ANKARANA

Iharana Bush Camp €€€€ *Near Réserve Spéciale d'Ankarana, tel: 032-1106296,* www.iharanabushcamp.com. Modelled on an East African safari camp, this rustically-luxurious lodge comprises 16 adobe suites decorated with white linen and colourful ethnic fabrics. Private balconies face a small bird-rich and rates include all meals and guided activities such as tsingy walks, boat trips and village visits. A swimming pool provides relief from the summer heat.

INDEX

Allée des Baobabs 52
Ambalavao 41
Ambositra 37
Antananarivo 26
  Croc Farm 31
  Gare Soarana 26
  Hôtel Colbert 27
  Jardin d'Andohalo 28
  Jardin
    d'Antaninarenina
    27
  Lac Anosy 28
  La Ferme d'Ivato 31
  Maison de Jean
    Laborde 28
  Marché Artisanal de
    la Digue 31
  Marché des Pavillons
    d'Analakely 26
  Musée
    d'Andafiavaratra
    28
  Musée d'Art et
    d'Archéologie 28
  Musée des Pirates 26
  Palais d'Ambohit
    sorohitra 27
  Palais de Justice
    d'Ambatondra
    fandrana 29
  Parc Botanique et
    Zoologique de
    Tsimbazaza 30
  Parc d'Ambohijatovo
    26
  Parc Tsarasaotra 30
  Place d'Andohalo 28
  Rova Ambohidrabiby
    32
  Rova Ambohimanga
    31

  Rova Antananarivo 29
  Rova Ilafy 32
  Tombeau de Rainiharo
    28
Antsirabe 36

Baie de Lokaro 49
Baie de Sainte Luce 49

Canal des Pangalanes 57
Chutes de la Lily 35
Circuit d'Anosiravo 75
Circuit de Tsimelahy 50

Diego Suarez 73
  Alliance Française 74
  Military Cemetery 74
  Nosy Lonjo 74
  Place Foch 73
  Place Joffre 74
  War Cemetery 74
Domaine de la Cascade
  50

Evatraha Peninsula 49

Fianarantsoa 40
Forêt de Baobabs 45
Fort d'Anosiravo 75
Fort Dauphin 46
  Musée du Fort
    Flacourt 47
  Plage d'Ankoba 47
  Plage de Libanona 47
Foulpointe 61

Geysers
  d'Andranomandraotra
  35

History 23

Ifaty 45
Iharana Massif 81
Île au Coq 59
Île aux Nattes 65
Île aux Prunes 60
Île Sainte-Marie 63
  Ambodifotatra 64
  Baie d'Ampanihy 65
  Cimetière des Pirates
    65
  Eglise Notre-Dame-
    de-l'Assomption 64
  Îlot Madame 64
  Vohilava 65
Îlot Sacré Ambohiniazy 35

Joffreville 77

Lac Ampitabe 58
Lac Itasy 35
Lac Lanirano 49
Lac Rasoabe 58
Lac Rasoamasay 58
Lac Sahambavy 40
La Mer d'Emeraude 76
Lemurs' Park 34

Mahajanga 55
  Cirque Rouge 55
  Musée Mozea Akiba 55
  Plage du Grand
    Pavois 55
  Villa Gustave Eiffel 55
Mahamasina 81
Mahambo 62
Manafiafy Lodge 49
Manakara 39
Manambato 58
Mandrare River Lodge 51
Mandrare River Valley 51
Mangily 45

Maroantsetra 65
Montagne des Français 75
Morondava 52

Nosy Be 67
    Ambaro 70
    Ambatoloaka 69
    Ambondrona 69
    Ampangorina 71
    Antagnianaomby 72
    Arbre Sacré de
        Mahatsinjo 68
    Bemoko 70
    Dzamandzary 69
    Espace Zeny 69
    Hell-Ville 68
    Lemuria Land 71
    Madirokely 69
    Mont Passot 70
    Nosy Iranja 72
    Nosy Komba 71
    Nosy Sakatia 72
    Nosy Tsarabanjina 72
    Parc National Marin
        de Nosy Tanikely 72
    Réserve Naturelle
        Intégrale de
        Lokobe 71

Palmarium Hotel 59
Parc Botanique de
    Saïadi 47
Parc Mitsinjo 33
Parc Musa 45
Parc National Andasibe-
    Mantadia 32
Parc National
    d'Andohahela 50
Parc National
    d'Andringitra 42
Parc National
    d'Ankarafantsika 56
Parc National de la
    Montagne d'Ambre 77
Parc National de l'Isalo
    43
Parc National de
    Mantadia 34
Parc National de Masoala
    66
Parc National de
    Ranomafana 38
Parc National des Tsingy
    de Bemaraha 53
Parc Voi MMA 33
Parc Zoologique Ivoloina
    60

Pays Zafimaniry 37
Pic St Louis 50

Ramena 76
Réserve d'Anja 41
Réserve de Bérenty 51
Réserve de Nahampoana
    48
Réserve de Reniala 45
Réserve de Vohibola 58
Réserve Forestière
    Kirindy 53
Réserve Spéciale
    d'Ankarana 79
Réserve Spéciale de Nosy
    Mangabe 66

Sainte Luce Reserve 49
Site Communautaire des
    Tsingy Rouges 78
Soatanana 38

Toamasina 59
Toliara 43
    Arboretum d'Antsokay
        44
    Musée Cedratom 44
    Musée de la Mer 44

INSIGHT ⊙ GUIDES POCKET GUIDE

MADAGASCAR

First edition 2019

Editor: Tatiana Wilde
Author: Philip Briggs
Head of DTP and Pre-Press: Daniel May
Picture Editor: Aude Vauconsant
Cartography: Carte
Photography Credits: Alamy 5T, 7R, 20, 91; Getty Images 16, 36, 68, 95, 97, 99, 104; iStock 1, 4TC, 4MC, 4TL, 5MC, 5M, 5M, 6L, 6R, 7, 11, 13, 15, 19, 29, 30, 33, 35, 39, 41, 42, 47, 48, 51, 53, 54, 57, 61, 64, 72, 77, 78, 79, 81, 82, 84, 86, 88, 100, 101, 103; Shutterstock 4ML, 5TC, 5MC, 24, 27, 45, 58, 62, 67, 70, 75, 89, 92
Cover Picture: iStock

Distribution
UK, Ireland and Europe: Apa Publications (UK) Ltd; sales@insightguides.com
United States and Canada: Ingram Publisher Services; ips@ingramcontent.com
Australia and New Zealand: Woodslane; info@woodslane.com.au
Southeast Asia: Apa Publications (SN) Pte; singaporeoffice@insightguides.com
Worldwide: Apa Publications (UK) Ltd; sales@insightguides.com

Special Sales, Content Licensing and CoPublishing
Insigh...
quant...
creat...

and corporate imprints tailored to your needs. sales@insightguides.com; www.insightguides.biz

All Rights Reserved
© 2019 Apa Digital (CH) AG and Apa Publications (UK) Ltd

Printed in China by CTPS

No part of this book may be reproduced, stored in a retrieval system or transmitted in any form or means electronic, mechanical, photocopying, recording or otherwise, without prior written permission from Apa Publications.

Contact us
Every effort has been made to provide accurate information in this publication, but changes are inevitable. The publisher cannot be responsible for any resulting loss, inconvenience or injury. We would appreciate it if readers would call our attention to any errors or outdated information. We also welcome your suggestions; please contact us at: hello@insightguides.com
www.insightguides.com